ADOLESCENT
PROBLEMS

The Emotional Literacy Handbook
Promoting Whole-School Strategies
Antidote
1-84312-060-7

Get Their Attention!
How to Gain Pupils' Respect and Thrive as a Teacher
Sean O'Flynn, Harry Kennedy and Michelle MacGrath
1-84312-080-1

How to Stop Bullying ... Towards a Non-Violent School
A Guide for Teachers and Support Staff
George Varnava
1-85346-938-6

An A to Z Practical Guide to Emotional and Behavioural Difficulties
Harry Ayers and Cesia Prytys
1-85346-778-2

Changing Behaviour
Teaching Children with Emotional and Behavioural Difficulties in Primary and
Secondary Classrooms (2nd edition)
Sylvia McNamara and Gill Moreton
1-85346-745-6

Individual Counselling Theory and Practice
A Reference Guide
Doula Nicolson and Harry Ayers
1-85346-373-6

ADOLESCENT PROBLEMS

A Practical Guide for Parents, Teachers and Counsellors

DOULA NICOLSON AND HARRY AYERS

Revised Edition

David Fulton Publishers

David Fulton Publishers Ltd
The Chiswick Centre, 414 Chiswick High Road, London W4 5TF

David Fulton Publishers is a division of Granada Learning.
First published in Great Britain by David Fulton Publishers 1997

Second edition 2004

10 9 8 7 6 5 4 3 2 1

Note: The right of Doula Nicolson and Harry Ayers to be identified as the authors of this work has been asserted by them in accordance with the Copyright, Designs and Patents Act 1988.

Copyright © Doula Nicolson and Harry Ayers 1997 and 2004

British Library Cataloguing in Publication Data
A catalogue record for this book is available from the British Library.

ISBN 1–84312–140–9

Typeset by RefineCatch Ltd., Bungay, Suffolk
Printed in Great Britain by Thanet Press

Contents

CHAPTER 1

Adolescent problems

This introductory book is intended to be a concise, structured, readable and eclectic reference **guide to theory and practice** with respect to **adolescent emotional and behavioural problems**. It should prove most useful for teachers, parents and all those who deal with and study adolescent problems, and also for adolescents themselves.

This guide includes **theories of adolescent development, theoretical and practical approaches to adolescent problems,** detailed sections on **common adolescent problems, counselling interview sheets** and **addresses and phone numbers of organisations** that can help with adolescent problems.

The main approaches included in the guide are **behavioural, cognitive, social learning, psychodynamic, person-centred** and **ecosystemic**, chosen because they are quite frequently used by practitioners.

The biological approach is also mentioned but not in any detail as this approach involves drug therapy which is the province of physicians and psychiatrists. It is worth stating that emotional and behavioural problems can result from physical conditions and the side-effects of drugs. Where this is suspected, it is advisable to consult a GP. It can also be the case that emotional and behavioural problems are symptomatic of a psychiatric disorder or the onset of such a disorder, and again, it is advisable to consult a GP.

Certain **issues and controversies** that fall outside the remit of this book do arise from time to time and need to be considered. For example:

- the **influence of heredity and the environment** on emotional and behavioural problems, i.e. how far there is a biological and genetic basis for such problems;
- whether a problem should be seen as **categorical**, i.e. a distinct, discrete category or **dimensional**, i.e. as lying along a continuum;
- how far these problems are the results of **traits or states** or an **interaction** between the two, e.g. temperament and situations;

- the **validity and the reliability of the assessment** of emotional and behavioural problems and the prevalence of such problems;
- the **influence of culture and ethnicity** on how problems are perceived and assessed;
- the **relative effectiveness of the different approaches** with respect to such problems.

The concept of adolescence

Adolescence is a **transitional stage** between childhood and adulthood. It is a period of biological, social, emotional and cognitive development which, if not negotiated satisfactorily, can lead to emotional and behavioural problems in adult life. It is customarily defined as **beginning at approximately 10 to 13** years of age and **ending between 18 and 22** years of age. It is usually subdivided into early and late adolescence.

Particular psychological and psychiatric problems can have their onset in adolescence or become more prevalent or noticeable during adolescence, e.g. phobias, anxiety, depression, suicide and attempted suicide, attention-deficit disorders, anorexia and bulimia, conduct disorders, schizophrenia and substance abuse.

Adolescence is also a time when adolescents strive to create their own personal identities and sense of autonomy which may at times lead to major or minor, temporary or permanent disagreements with their parents, carers or teachers. Most adolescents negotiate this phase satisfactorily and enjoy positive relationships with their parents and other adults.

Adolescence can be viewed from different developmental perspectives. It can be seen as being influenced by a variety of factors: genetic, temperamental and environmental. Puberty begins during adolescence, a period of hormonal and bodily changes which in turn are associated with psychological changes. Adolescents can become preoccupied with bodily image and physical attractiveness, particularly in relation to their peers or in relation to media models or ideals. They may be early or late maturers and as one or the other may experience particular problems, e.g. fears and doubts about what is normal development for their age. Additionally, they may engage in risky behaviour and be catapulted into early adulthood.

Cognitively, adolescence is a time when, in Piagetian terms, adolescents should reach the formal operational stage which means that they should be able to reason logically and abstractly, consider hypothetical possibilities and engage in problem-solving activities. They should also be able to engage in meta-cognition, i.e. reflecting on their own cognitive processes. There is also a tendency to compare themselves with their peers and to what they perceive as ideal standards; this may lead them to become self-conscious and this can adversely affect their self-esteem, particularly with regard to their own perceived lack of physical attractiveness. Low self-esteem may contribute to particular problems, e.g. loneliness, depression, suicide, anorexia and conduct disorders. They may try out different roles on their way to forming a sense of personal identity. Adolescents also have fantasies about themselves and their futures.

In terms of social cognition, adolescence is a time when adolescents reason about themselves and their social world. This means that adolescents become egocentric, thinking others, either imaginary or real, are as interested in them as they are in themselves. There is an emphasis on how others see them and a desire to be noticed and recognised. Adolescents also develop perspective-taking and, if successful, come to understand the thoughts and feelings of others.

They may become idealistic and interested in religious, philosophical and political ideas and movements. As a result, the adult world may appear to them to be hypocritical and immoral.

Psychodynamically, adolescence is a time when adolescents strive to develop independence and to distance themselves from their parents. They begin to form a personal and sexual identity of their own. It is also a period when childhood trauma may surface and when adolescents become aware of unconscious conflicts.

The significance of adolescence lies in the fact that, along with childhood, it provides the foundation for adulthood.

Theories of adolescent development

Erikson

His analysis of the period of adolescence focuses on the **concept of identity**. He defines identity as being composed of a genetic inheritance together with a particular way of organising experience that is in turn structured by a given cultural context. Personal identity is therefore partly determined by the individual's psychological make-up but also by the community of which that individual is a part. That identity is one that is both conscious and unconscious, providing a sense of continuity. It is rooted in a past that helps shape the future.

Identity evolves throughout childhood by the processes of **introjection** (internalising the persona of significant others) and **identification** (assimilating the roles and values of others). Personal identity also depends on the way society responds. Identity formation occurs when the adolescent chooses from a variety of introjections and identifications and achieves a new synthesis. This identity formation continues throughout the life of the individual.

Erikson believes that human development adheres to the **principle of epigenesis** which means that everything emerges from a basic 'ground plan' in parts, with each part experiencing a period of ascendancy, finally forming an integrated whole. He outlines **eight stages of development**, each stage being conflictual and having the possibility of two opposing, **bipolar outcomes**. Individuals experience conflicting possibilities and if they resolve these conflicts, a positive self-concept is formed. But if the conflict persists or is unresolved, then a negative or **dystonic element** is incorporated into a person's identity, leading to a negative self-concept and psychological problems. However, he states that both **syntonic** (positive) and **dystonic** are necessary for there to be satisfactory personal adaptation. Identity issues are never finally resolved and may be affected by role changes and major life events, depending on changing needs and circumstances. Optimal identity formation should include a commitment to roles, values and sexual orientation that reflect an individual's particular abilities and needs.

Erikson states that the fifth stage is the one that characterises the period of adolescence. It is the stage of **identity versus role confusion**. The individual is faced with achieving a synthesis through transcending childhood identifications and undertaking expected social roles. The adolescent should achieve a balance between the bipolar outcomes, thus enabling the individual to adapt to his or her environment. Prior to this fifth stage the adolescent will have passed through four other necessary stages:

- trust versus mistrust;
- autonomy versus shame and doubt;
- initiative versus guilt;
- industry versus inferiority.

Erikson believes it is necessary for the infant to develop a balance of trust and mistrust in order to navigate the world securely. Mutual recognition and mutual trustworthiness form the bases for a future sense of personal identity. Mistrust alone is dystonic and may result in identity confusion in adolescence and thereby lead to a sense of alienation from others.

Autonomy means acquiring a sense of self-control; this self-control may be achieved through conflict manifested in disobedience. Successful resolution of this stage will lead the child to develop a desire to be him- or herself which becomes a necessary precondition for attaining personal identity in adolescence. The dystonic result could be self-doubt and dependency leading to the avoidance of difficult situations or, alternatively, defiance of parents and authority in general.

If the child develops initiative at this stage, this sets the scene for experimenting with different social and sexual roles in adolescence. If children are constrained by parents in their exploration and initiative-taking, then they may be inhibited by guilt and fear, thus restricting themselves to fixed roles and over-dependency on adults.

The stage between starting secondary school and puberty is referred to as the **apprenticeship for life**, where a positive attitude to work is acquired through identification with role models who possess and display knowledge and skills. Work is the stage where the child builds a desire for achievement and feelings of competence. If this stage is not satisfactorily negotiated, the child will feel incompetent, inferior and experience **work paralysis** and futility.

For Erikson, adolescence is the period when individuals must form a personal identity and avoid role diffusion and identity confusion. The adolescent must address a number of identity questions: 'Where do I originate from?', 'Who am I?' and 'What do I want to be?' The goal is to achieve an integrated synthesis of past, present and future which together contribute to an adolescent's identity. This identity is also the product of reciprocal interaction between the individual and significant others, i.e. peer group and role models. The adolescent also needs to come to terms with physical changes and sexual desire. If personal identity is poorly formed, the risks of delinquency and psychological problems can arise. These problems can emerge due to past difficulties with mistrust, shame, doubt, guilt and feelings of inferiority.

Adolescent love is seen by Erikson as primarily a means by which adolescents test out their evolving identity through redefinition and revision of their self-concept. The adolescent is also concerned to establish vocational goals and initially aims to achieve often unrealistic and idealised occupational roles, particularly ones that 'heroes' possess. Adolescent identification is often with such 'heroes' in preference to their parents whom they rebel against. Erikson sees such rebellion as the adolescent striving to achieve autonomy and independence and thereby form a separate identity. The adolescent pursues **fidelity** which is the quest for something to identify with and be identified by: a step on the way to attaining autonomy.

The attainment of personal identity also requires the adolescent to develop a philosophy of life that will provide a means by which life events can be evaluated. If the adolescent fails to achieve a sense of personal identity, then self-doubt, role diffusion and confusion will lead to subservience to or alienation from others. If prolonged, then delinquency or psychological disorders may occur. Crises particularly arise at transition points from child to adult status and from dependence on parents to independence.

Marcia has elaborated on Erikson's stage of adolescence. He refers to **crisis/exploration and commitment**. Crisis/exploration is where the adolescent explores identity problems and critically examines parental norms in order to consider viable alternatives. Commitment is where the individual decides on his or her level of adherence to chosen goals and values. The absence or presence of these two criteria determine Marcia's four separate modes for outlining adolescent identity issues.

- **The identity-diffused or identity-confused individual**: this adolescent has not yet considered identity issues or has not satisfactorily resolved such issues; consequently, this individual may drift aimlessly, become manipulative or self-centred.
- **The foreclosure individual** is unreflectively committed and has identified with parents and significant others but has not yet engaged in exploration or experienced an identity crisis; consequently, this individual may become intolerant of others who are different.
- **The moratorium individual** is in crisis and is striving to achieve a personal identity through experimenting with different roles and values but remains uncommitted or has only achieved a tenuous commitment; consequently, the individual will challenge convention and desire to question and change existing institutions but often fail to present realistic alternatives.
- **The identity-achieved individual** has achieved a self-chosen identity through

exploration and is committed to a value system; consequently, the individual has achieved continuity and stability and has come to accept his or her self-concept and commitments.

This typology is not meant to be rigid as each mode is seen as a continuing process. The modes do not form inevitable stages moving from one to another and the moratorium is the only stage that is a precondition for the attainment of identity due to its emphasis on exploration. Identity is never final because roles change and, as a result, identity issues may re-emerge.

Kohlberg

Kohlberg sees the development of moral reasoning as an aspect of the formation of personal identity. His approach is based on Piaget's investigation into children's moral thinking; in particular on Piaget's point that two kinds of moral reasoning are associated with particular stages of cognitive development. Children who are at the **pre-operational** level display **moral realism**, i.e. they judge the rightness of an action by its consequences, not by people's intentions, and also see rules as unchangeable. When children move to the stage of **concrete operations**, they consider people's intentions and believe that rules can be arbitrary and changeable. This is the stage of **moral relativism**.

Kohlberg examines the moral reasoning behind judgements arrived at concerning certain moral dilemmas. He suggests six hierarchical stages in the development of moral reasoning which are included within three levels of judgement. These stages are invariant and reflect increasing internalisation of principles.

The moral reasoning stages are:

pre-conventional (pre-moral), conventional (moral) and **post-conventional (autonomous)** levels. Each of these levels in turn is divided into two stages.

Level 1   Pre-conventional or pre-moral

Most commonly occurs between ages 4 to 10 but can be displayed by adolescents and adults. Moral reasoning at this level is self-centred, based on expectations of reward or fear of punishment.

Level 1, Stage 1   Heteronomous morality

At this level children define right and wrong in terms of obedience and disobedience to authorities. People are valued in terms of their power and status and also their ability to dispense rewards and punishments.

Level 1, Stage 2   Instrumental morality

At this point children decide that what is right or wrong depends on what personal needs are satisfied. They think of ways in which they can get others to reward them; this may lead them to consider the needs of others but only as a means of achieving their own ends.

Level 2, Stage 2   Conventional or moral

Children at this level wish to meet social expectations and, as a result, accept the existing order of things. Most adolescents and adults function at this level.

Level 2, Stage 3   Interpersonal conformity

Children at this level see being good as gaining the approval of others; being wrong as receiving the disapproval of others. They conform to peer group norms or those of significant others. They also judge people's actions by their intentions. Kohlberg states that females remain at this stage longer than males, a view challenged by Gilligan (1977). Gilligan states that sex differences in moral reasoning exist but that they are complementary, not inferior or superior. Women base their morality on caring for others, sensitivity to others' needs and interpersonal relationships whereas men base morality on abstract principles of justice and rights.

Level 2, Stage 4   Social system and morality

At this stage there is a strong belief in the legal system and authority. These are seen as fixed and unchangeable and supported for fear of breakdown in law and order if they should be challenged. The law is observed through fear and guilt and in order to avoid punishment for wrongdoing.

Level 3   Post-conventional or autonomous level

Individuals choose their own moral principles which are no longer based on selfishness, approval from others or conformity to the status quo.

Level 3, Stage 5   Human rights

Moral reasoning at this level is based on the ideas of human rights, equality before the law and mutual obligations. Individuals engage in reasoning based on concern for the common good. Unjust rules need to be changed. Laws can be changed as long as the changes are based on rational discussion and consensus.

Level 3, Stage 6   Morality of ethical principles

This highest stage is based on the overarching principles of human dignity and equality. Laws that infringe such principles have to be broken but punishment for breaking them has to be accepted. Civil disobedience may be undertaken where ethical principles provide justification; however, the individual has to prove to society that such principles override those laws by accepting punishment.

Loevinger

Loevinger's approach is based on empirical evidence and statistical analysis. Her concept of the ego is one where there is a general framework in which meaning and coherence are produced. Her notion of ego development sees internal conflict inherent at all stages and variability of ego stages within the same age range. The ego is seen as developing through invariant and hierarchical stages.

The ego stages

Adolescents can be discovered in most stages.

Stages

1–1   Pre-social symbiotic

0–0   Pre-social phase

Infants are preoccupied with gratification of their own needs and discovering their self as against their not-self. Those unable to distinguish between self and not-self are described as autistic.

1–1   Symbiotic phase

Infants manifest a strong dependence on their mothers but still cannot distinguish between self and mother. An adolescent at this stage would not be integrated into society but be marginalised.

1–2   Impulsive

Particularly found in early childhood but rare in adolescence. Others are seen purely as sources of material rewards. Self-control is weak and is only attainable through immediate gratification or fear of punishment.
People are seen as either useful or obstructive. There is a preoccupation with sexual and aggressive feelings. The adolescent delinquent functions at this stage.

1–2   Self-protective

Self-control begins to appear. There arises a wish to control, manipulate and dominate others. Individuals fear being caught and blame others for their plight rather than accept any responsibility. They tend to be suspicious of others because of that wish to control them.

1–3   Conformist

This is the period of early adolescence. They display conformity because they are concerned to gain the approval and acceptance of others. There is a preoccupation with their image in the eyes of others and as a consequence importance is attached to physical appearance and being sociable. Material possessions become very important. People are judged by appearance and possessions. There is a great desire to belong to the in-group. Reasoning is based on platitudes and stereotypes.

1–3/4   Self-awareness

This is a transitional stage also called the 'conscientious-conformist level'. Young people are becoming aware of differences and develop concerns over individuality, femininity and masculinity. Individuals see value judgements as needing to be related to contexts. They become critical of themselves, aware of not meeting others' expectations and as a result may feel guilty, isolated and self-conscious.

1–4   Conscientious

At this stage the individual develops internalised moral principles. There is a greater concentration on motives and feelings. People are seen as having individual needs and differences and tolerance of those differences emerges. The individual expands a sense of responsibility from family and peer group to society as a whole. Work is seen as providing opportunities for personal enrichment, not as a burdensome chore. Behaviour is now more consistent and stable. This stage of development is characteristic of late adolescence.

1–4/5   Individualistic

There is further growth in terms of tolerance for individual differences and in the awareness that people undertake a variety of different roles. This level is found among more mature late adolescents.

1–5   Autonomous

These individuals display greater self-control and are able to cope with ambiguity and internal conflicts.

1–6   Integrated

These individuals have attained a strong sense of identity and have developed a desire to improve themselves and society. They have evaluated themselves and are aware of their weaknesses and limits. They assume responsibility for their beliefs and behaviour. This stage corresponds to Maslow's notion of the self-actualising person. Loevinger sees the attainment of this stage as very rare.

Adolescents span the range from self-protective to individualistic but rarely come under the pre-conformist, autonomous or integrated stages. Most come between the conformist and conscientious stages. The actual rate of ego development depends on the particular individual. Specific ages are not related to any of the particular stages but there are general connections. Each stage builds on the previous one, including elements of that stage as well as changing those elements. The individual level of ego maturity is assessed through the use of a 36-item Sentence Completion Test but this can only commence with the threshold of the impulsive stage when language is sufficiently developed. Higher stages of ego development are not seen as superior or healthier. An individual at any stage could be maladjusted or not.

Bandura

Bandura's **social cognitive approach** is based on the idea of analysing reciprocal interactions between people and their environment. People are seen as active agents who are able to construct cognitive or symbolic representations of events. They are also pictured as being influenced by external events. The process of **reciprocal determinism** is triadic. It is a process whereby three factors reciprocally influence each other.

These three factors are:

> E: **the external environment;**
> B: **the acquired behaviour;**
> P: **the person in terms of their genetic predispositions, cognition, intelligence, motivation, self-efficacy, self-concept and beliefs.**

A person's neurological and physiological constitution (P) constrains the kinds of behaviour (B) that are possible but these in turn can be modified through the efforts of the individual.

P influences B and B influences P.

An individual's attitudes and beliefs (P) can influence his or her social environment (E) and in turn social environment can modify the person's attitudes and beliefs.

P influences E and E influences P.

Finally, the environment (E) is changed by a person's behaviour (B) and reciprocally a person's behaviour is influenced by his or her environment.

E influences B and B influences E.

People are not entirely free of environmental influence but within limits are able to make choices and achieve goals through exercising self-control.

This process can be identified in adulthood as well as adolescence and therefore in that sense there is no separate stage called adolescence. Social cognitive theory does not subscribe to the idea of developmental stages. What marks adolescence is the social and cultural pressures, attitudes and expectations that influence adolescents. Social learning theory encompasses both social influences and cognitive processes, particularly that of self-regulation. The following elements of social cognitive theory are ones that can be used to characterise any age.

Vicarious reinforcement

People can observe others and see what happens to them in terms of positive and negative consequences. Seeing others being reinforced or punished for specific behaviours can lead to imitation of or avoidance of those behaviours. For example, individuals may adopt certain types of language, dress, roles and relationships if they think these will be rewarded by their peers or encouragement is received through the media.

● **Attention**

The ages and cognitive levels of individuals help to determine the amount of attention paid to an observed model. Other variables also affect particular individuals' level of attention. Among these are:

- the desirable attributes of the model and the way they are presented;
- whether the environment reinforces or punishes their behaviours;
- their past experiences with a similar model;
- particular circumstances or cues that focus their attention.

- **Retention**

For individuals to remember, they must possess sufficient capacity to encode, store and recall information if they are going to be able to learn from an observed model.

- **Reproducing behaviour**

Individuals must have a repertoire of skills (cognitive, social and motoric) if they are going successfully to reproduce behaviours observed.

- **Motivation**

If individuals are going to reproduce the observed behaviours they must be motivated. This may happen through:

vicarious reinforcement	seeing others experience positive consequences from performing particular behaviours;
direct reinforcement	having their own behaviours rewarded;
observational learning	imitating others' appropriate and inappropriate behaviours because they are seen as having status or as being right.

Symbolic processes

This approach emphasises the social aspects of learning a language, namely the imitation and observation by adolescents of others who use it.

Anticipatory processes

The emphasis here is on adolescents imagining or predicting what might happen in the present or in the future. These imaginings can motivate the adolescent to perform specific behaviours to achieve desired goals.

Self-regulation ability

This ability is necessary for adolescents to set targets for themselves, to motivate themselves and to evaluate their activities in terms of success and failure. External influences have a bearing on adolescent behaviour even when self-regulation is exercised.

Self-reflecting ability

This ability is made up of four elements: comparing one's performance with one's goals; comparing different ways of reaching those goals and their social consequences; reflecting on the most efficient ways of reaching those goals; and gauging one's ability to assess how capable one is of achieving one's goals (termed **self-efficacy**).

Self-efficacy

This term refers to one's estimation of how far one can achieve a given goal. If adolescents have a high level of confidence in their ability to achieve their goals, i.e. high perceived self-efficacy, this will enable them to increase their attainments.

Self-efficacy is enhanced by past successes, seeing others succeed who have similar abilities, being encouraged by others and being realistic about one's capabilities.

A distinction is made between efficacy expectation which is the belief that one has the ability to perform a particular task and outcome expectation which is assessing correctly that particular actions will result in specific outcomes.

Self-reinforcement

Adolescents can be taught to reinforce themselves when they perform a task well. They can set an appropriate level of performance which when attained will provide encouragement in setting even higher levels, thus increasing their feelings of self-worth. This process of self-reinforcement is seen as being more effective than external reinforcement.

Modelling

Modelling refers to the practice of demonstrating particular behaviours which others learn through imitation. Modelling can have a positive or negative, inhibiting or uninhibiting, effect on an observer, e.g. an adolescent may imitate his or her peers' social or anti-social behaviour, such as substance abuse. This may be particularly the case where the behaviour has a high status in some adolescent peer groups.

At particular stages certain role models might be imitated, e.g. parents, peers, media people and sports stars. The imitation of these role models may wax and wane depending on factors like age, gender, times of transition and moments of crisis.

Social cognitive

There has been a move from depending solely on imitation and modelling to explain social learning. This has meant Bandura considering the role of cognitive processes in imitating others.

This approach to adolescence considers as paramount the influence of the social situations that adolescents find themselves in rather than the age of adolescents. There is an emphasis on the influence of social, cultural and subcultural expectations on adolescent behaviour. Positive adolescent behaviour is seen as more the norm than not and as being the result of particular child-rearing practices and parent–child relationships.

This approach assumes that social situations have more bearing on behaviour than the maturational influences. New behaviours can best be explained as originating from observational learning *per se* rather than simply through reinforcement. A distinction is made between acquiring responses and the actual performing of those responses. Whether responses occur depend largely on the particular combination of social situations and cognitive processes. Responses although learned may remain dormant until elicited or deemed appropriate.

Aggression is seen from this perspective as a product of social influences, in particular, the imitation of aggressive parents. Parents are seen as socialising children through adequate and consistent contact of the right kind and through meeting their dependency needs. If dependency needs are ignored, then the child may become hostile. Parents of aggressive boys tend to be more punitive and use corporal punishment to instil obedience and thereby encourage their sons to use aggression as a means of resolving conflict outside the home.

With regard to the influence of TV on behaviour, it is claimed that children who extensively watch aggressive behaviour on TV become engaged in more aggressive behaviour. It also results in those children becoming more insensitive to violence over time and therefore making aggression more acceptable as a means of solving problems. Heavy TV watching may be a reaction to the difficulties that some children find in developing and sustaining friendships and to the lack of school achievement.

Bronfenbrenner

His analysis of adolescent development is based on an ecological approach which understands adolescents in terms of their relationships with one another and their changing social and environmental contexts or systems. His approach is based on **Lewin's Field Theory** which sees behaviour as a function or interaction between the individual and their environment. Analogously, for Bronfenbrenner, adolescent development is the result of an interaction between the individual and his or her environment. Change in the surrounding physical environment and in the social environment impacts on an adolescent's development. He calls this a **Process-Person-Context Model**. He defines the environment as consisting of four inter-related systems:

- **The microsystem** is the immediate, face-to-face system of interpersonal interactions, a social network of relationships, e.g. the family, peer groups, neighbours and school. The influence of such systems on the adolescent may increase or decrease. The peer group may come to have a predominant influence either positively or negatively. Positive adolescent development depends on mutual reciprocity between parents and adolescents.

- **The mesosystem** consists of the interactions between different microsystems, e.g. adolescent and parents and adolescent and peer group. A typical adolescent has many different roles which vary over time and across different contexts. Age segregation has intensified and as a result relationships between some parents and adolescents have weakened and adolescents are perceived as more problematic than in the past. Effective communication and interactions between parents and adolescents are seen as necessary for positive adolescent development. For there to be maximal positive development, the different microsystems need to be in harmony or congruent with each other.

- **The ecosystem** is the local community to which the adolescent belongs, e.g. school and neighbourhoods, the local authority and work. Changes in these subsystems may affect adolescents and influence their behaviour.

- **The macrosystem** is the whole system which incorporates the micro-, meso- and ecosystem together with the social and cultural values that inform that system. These values define what constitutes adolescence and also an adolescent's social and legal status.

Problems may arise if:

- There are few or no interactions and communication between microsystems, e.g. if parents and adolescents are isolated from each other or if adolescents are isolated from one another.

- There are no or few areas of agreement over values, e.g. peer groups and parents may disagree over what is acceptable behaviour. This may lead to internal conflict in the adolescent, resulting in outright rejection of parental values or a continuing state of mental tension.

- There is encouragement from different microsystems for adolescents to engage in deviant or delinquent behaviour which leads to adolescents being in conflict with the law.

Ecological transition

This concept refers to major changes in the constitutive subsystems or the system as a whole. Changes in and between microsystems lead to changing roles, e.g. moving schools and parental divorce. Changes in the macrosystem may also lead to ecological transitions.

Blos

Blos adopts a **psychoanalytic and object relations** view of adolescent development. He looks at adolescence in classical terms of the resolution of the Oedipal complex and also in terms of pre-Oedipal conflicts.

He maintains that there are **four challenges** which face adolescents:

- **the second individuation process**, i.e. the letting-go of internalised parental structures;
- **coping with childhood trauma**, i.e. re-experiencing the damage inflicted by past traumas so as to control it;
- **ego continuity**, i.e. having a sense of personal continuity linking the past with the present;
- **sexual identity**, i.e. the need to develop a sense of sexual identity.

The role of regression in his approach is seen as normative in that it enables an adolescent to disengage from past object relations.

Second individuation process

The adolescent needs to develop a mature ego; for this to occur there has to be disengagement from the internalised representations of the parents. This process enables adolescents to develop their own identities independent of their parents. For adolescents to achieve this goal successfully they have to recontact their old infantile desires. These regressive behaviours take the form of expressing themselves in terms of actions rather than words, idolising media stars, immersing themselves. Regression is the reaction to the loss of internal objects which provided support. Often adolescents resort to peer group support to cope with the painful loss of internal parental representations. This loss leads to a process of mourning for those objects.

Adolescents can attempt to resolve these separation and individuation challenges by evasion, e.g. by distancing themselves from their parents either physically or ideologically.

Coping with childhood trauma

Coping with childhood emotional trauma is never complete but in adolescence a considerable part of this task is undertaken. The aim is to integrate the trauma into the ego and as each effort succeeds, the adolescent raises his or her self-esteem. Avoidance of this task can lead to negative effects, e.g. in terms of phobias and compulsive behaviour.

Ego continuity

It is necessary for adolescents to develop a sense of ego continuity connecting the present with the past. It enables an adolescent to mature without the necessity of internalised parental representations.

Sexual identity

The adolescent needs to achieve a sense of being masculine or feminine. This sexual identity is attained through the adolescent resolving Oedipal conflicts. Preoccupation with heterosexuality may be one way the adolescent copes with sexual feelings towards the same-sex parent. An adolescent who continues to sustain such feelings towards the same-sex parent may inhibit the development of heterosexuality. By resolving Oedipal conflicts arising from feelings for the same-sex parent the adolescent develops a mature ego-ideal.

Personality or character formation

There are five stages of development through which the challenges above are faced:

- **The latency stage** occurs before adolescence and is an opportunity for the ego and superego to master biological desires.

- **Pre-adolescence** is a time where there is an upsurge of sexual desire and aggression which the ego finds difficult to control. Attempts to satisfy these drives directly meet with the censure of the superego. The anxiety aroused by these conflicts generates defence mechanisms, e.g. repression, displacement, projection and reaction formation.

- **Early adolescence** is a phase where the adolescent reaches puberty and commences the process of separation from early object relationships. The sexual drive is now directed towards others outside the family. Superegos are weakened as the ego struggles to maintain control. Adolescents idealise their friendships, seeking in others desirable attributes they lack. Such idealisation can lead to abrupt termination of friendships resulting from adolescents feeling overwhelmed or fearing that they are becoming homosexual. When adolescence proper occurs, then adolescents leave behind Oedipal conflicts and an interest in other people emerges. This period of redirection is a time when adolescents can feel at sea and as a consequence they may engage in a hectic emotional life in order to cope with turmoil.

- **Late adolescence** is a time when adolescents finally form a stable sexual identity and attain definite self-images and images of others. They have acquired a sense of autonomy, seeing themselves as separate people in their own right.

- **Post-adolescence** is the transition stage when the adolescent becomes a mature adult. The tasks of this transition period are to discover socially acceptable outlets through which their biological drives and their resolutions of childhood traumas can be directed.

Kegan

Identity formation

Kegan sees the adolescent as forging an identity through a process of making or creating meaning. This process is one which constantly reconstructs the subject–object relationship. The boundaries between self and object are formed and reformed and in this way adolescents form and reform their identities. What was once subject becomes object. What the individual once was the individual now has.

Stage 0   Growth and loss of the incorporative self

The infant is simply the reflexes and drives that it experiences through its self. There is no awareness of an external world existing apart from the self. There is no self–object balance.

Stage 1   Growth and loss of the impulsive balance

The infant discovers that there is an external world separate from his or her self which he or she is not able to control or affect. There is no ability to take the view of another, there is no experience of ambivalence and the self and others are seen as either good or bad. The child finally gains control over his or her impulses and the impulsive self becomes an object of reflection for the child.

Stage 2   Growth and loss of the imperial balance

Children develop stable needs and stable behaviour. They become more autonomous and also realise that others have different views. The child's self is composed of his or her desires, wishes and needs but there is no reflection on those needs, thus the needs of others are not incorporated into the self.

Stage 3   Growth and loss of the interpersonal balance

Children are now able to reflect on their needs and incorporate the needs of others. The self, however, is its interpersonal relationships and therefore does not reflect on such relationships. The self has a need for the approval of others and therefore does not consider anything outside this mutually shared world.

Stage 4   Growth and loss of the institutional balance

This stage is where the individual has relationships as well as is his or her relationships. The self acquires meaning from the institution. Individuals become their livelihood, nationality and religion.

Stage 5   Growth of the inter-individual balance

The self has rather than is its institutional connections. Individuals have their livelihood, nationality and religion. Institutions are no longer seen as the ultimate goal; rather, the new self looks at ways institutions can meet individual objectives. The individual can stand apart from the institution and reflect on its purpose.

Theoretical approaches to adolescent problems

Biological approach

This approach seeks to look for connections between biology and behaviour, i.e.:

- that there are connections between an individual's organic states and his or her behavioural and emotional difficulties;
- that an individual's genetic make-up can interact with the environment and lead to that individual developing behavioural and emotional difficulties.

Behavioural genetics attempts to discover the relative contribution of heredity and the environment to differences or variability between individuals. This is undertaken through seeing if specific problems run in families and through twin studies and adoption studies.

This approach has arrived at the following conclusion:

> that many behavioural and emotional difficulties arise through an interaction between an individual's genetic predisposition and his or her environment, e.g. attention-deficit hyperactivity disorder.

Attention-Deficit Hyperactivity Disorder (ADHD)

This disorder is characterised as one where a child has a combination of some or all of the following attributes: developmentally inappropriate inattention, hyperactivity and impulsivity. It may have its beginning in infancy. Children with ADHD may manifest the following symptoms: hyperactivity, perceptual and motor problems, erratic feelings and moods, poor co-ordination, inattention, impulsivity, cognitive and memory problems, specific learning difficulties and problems with speech and hearing. A high proportion display aggressive behaviour. They can also display depression as a result of experiencing the disorder. In school they can show both learning and behavioural difficulties.

This disorder is defined as a medical condition and is believed to have a biological basis (a problem with neurotransmitters), a genetic component and as having three subtypes:

- mainly inattentive type;
- mainly hyperactive-impulsive type;
- combined type.

For this condition to be diagnosed, the behaviours must be observed in at least two settings, e.g. school and home. At school the child may have an associated reading and numeracy difficulty.

The course of the disorder is somewhat unpredictable in that it may persist into adolescence and adulthood or remit at puberty.

The condition is often treated by giving a child a psychostimulant drug called Ritalin (methylphenidate) and this drug therapy is often combined with behavioural and cognitive behavioural type interventions at home and in the classroom. This drug has been assessed as being effective with most children but can have side effects, e.g. headaches, stomach-aches, nausea and insomnia.

The biological approach also states:

- that it is important to study and therefore be aware of the different experiences adolescents have within the same family, including the different ways in which parents treat the same child and the different types of interactions between siblings, i.e. non-shared environments;
- adolescents, through their genetic make-up, influence how parents respond to them and as a result contribute to the formation of their own environment;
- for there to be optimal child development the parents' treatment of a child must match their particular child's hereditary make-up.

NB: This approach is mentioned simply so that teachers and parents are made aware that behavioural and emotional difficulties may result from medical or organic conditions and therefore it is necessary if this is suspected to consult a GP or psychiatrist.

Even where there is a medical or biological basis for behavioural and emotional difficulties, parents and teachers may still be able to make an impact on those difficulties.

Behavioural approach

This approach is based on the idea that adolescent emotional and behavioural difficulties are mainly the **product of learning experiences**.

It emphasises the **use of scientific methodology** in approaching the study of behaviour. This means constructing testable hypotheses about behaviour, concentrating on observable behaviour and being objective in describing that behaviour. This approach avoids speculation and high levels of inference about the causes of behaviour; instead it focuses on empirical findings.

The main assumptions underlying this approach are:

- Both **heredity and the environment interact** together to influence an adolescent's behaviour.

- An adolescent has a range of behaviours which arise from what he or she learns within and from particular social and physical environments. Thus, the focus is on external rather than internal influences on an adolescent's behaviour. The main aim of this approach is to manipulate those external influences in order to change an adolescent's behaviour.

- There are two main types of learning, i.e. **classical conditioning** and **operant conditioning**.

- Emotional and behavioural difficulties are in part the product of maladaptive learning experiences.

Classical conditioning (Pavlovian)

The theory of classical or respondent conditioning originates in the work of Ivan Pavlov. The essence of this theory is that a previously neutral stimulus becomes capable of bringing about a particular reaction because it has become paired with a stimulus that automatically produces the same or a similar reaction.

In the salivating dog experiment, the dog learns to salivate to the neutral stimulus (the bell) without presentation of food because the dog has been conditioned to salivate to the sound of the bell alone by the pairing of the bell with the food.

In the case of Albert, an 11-month-old child, he was conditioned to fear rats which previously he had not feared by pairing an aversive noise with the appearance of a rat.

Classical conditioning theory has been used to explain the origin of fears and phobias and has generated ways of treating these phobias and fears through:

- **Systematic desensitisation**: this involves constructing a hierarchy of anxiety producing situations according to the intensity of fear experienced. The phobic person is then taught relaxation techniques and after these have been learned works through the hierarchy, beginning with the least anxiety-producing situation first until he or she can cope with the most anxiety-producing situation.

- **Flooding**: this involves confronting the phobic person with the most anxiety-producing situation right from the beginning. The person is prevented from escaping or avoiding the aversive situation through physical or instructional response prevention.

Operant conditioning (Skinnerian)

The theory of operant conditioning originates in the work of Skinner. Operant conditioning theory relates an individual's overt, observable responses to environmental events. The individual emits responses (operants) and these responses are either reinforced or not by the environment. A reinforcer is an event (stimulus) that follows a response and increases the likelihood of it happening again. A reinforcer thereby strengthens the behaviour. What acts as a reinforcer for a particular individual has to be discovered empirically and cannot be determined beforehand.

Operant conditioning has been used to explain the origin of a wide range of behaviours and ways of treating emotional and behavioural difficulties.

- **Positive reinforcement** occurs where an adolescent is reinforced or rewarded for desired behaviour and can also occur when he or she is positively reinforced for undesired behaviour. This type of reinforcement, when administered, observably increases behaviours, desirable or not.

- **Shaping** occurs where there is reinforcement of successive approximations to the desired behaviour.

- **Extinction** occurs where reinforcement of a particular behaviour is stopped, leading to diminishing frequency of that behaviour.

- **Negative reinforcement** occurs where the removal of an unpleasant or aversive event leads to an increase in the likelihood of the preceding event. In escape learning an adolescent's responses increase because they are connected with the removal of unpleasant stimuli. Behaviour can be changed this way by applying an unpleasant shock to adolescents until they decide to end the shock by performing the desired behaviour. In avoidance learning, behaviours are reinforced because the adolescent avoids the unpleasant event.

- **Punishment** occurs where an aversive event occurs following the behaviour, leading to a decrease in that behaviour.

With regard to punishment, particular undesirable effects may occur:

- It encourages adolescents to find ways of escaping or avoiding punishment, sometimes through performing further undesirable behaviours.

- It can arouse the desire for revenge, leading to retaliatory behaviours.

- On its own, it does not guide the adolescent to what specific positive behaviours he or she should be adopting.

- It can often have only short-term effects and, once removed, can lead to the rapid reappearance of undesired behaviour.

- It can lead to physical abuse.

Therefore the operant approach generally discourages the use of punishment and relies instead on the use of positive reinforcement to encourage desired behaviours.

Behavioural assessment

This form of assessment follows a scientific methodology. This means there is an emphasis on observing overt and specific behaviours in particular settings or contexts, e.g. home, school and college. The aim is to reveal a pattern of behaviour, what events lead up to it (antecedents) and what events follow it (consequences), an **ABC** or **functional analysis**. By arriving at a representative sample of the behaviour in terms of its frequency and duration, it is possible to determine a baseline. This baseline can provide a means of comparing behaviour at the beginning of an intervention with the behaviour at the end of an intervention, enabling one to see whether there has been any improvement in behaviour.

The behavioural approach for teachers and parents

This approach is relatively easy to learn and to put into practice. It requires teachers and parents to concentrate on positively reinforcing an adolescent's appropriate behaviour and where possible ignoring minor misbehaviour. The idea is to shape an adolescent's behaviour in the direction the parent or teacher desires. The teacher or parent has to be vigilant and observant in order to note appropriate behaviour so as to reward or reinforce that behaviour.

The teacher and parent must be clear as to what target behaviours they expect the adolescent to achieve and ensure that the adolescent is also clear as to what is expected. These targets should be – as far as possible – specific, measurable, achievable, relevant and time-related (SMART).

Rewards or reinforcers are only such if they have the desired effect of increasing the desired behaviour. The parent and teacher need to work out what the adolescent finds reinforcing or rewarding and not assume they know already. The reinforcers do not necessarily have to be material, e.g. money or goods; they can be non-material, e.g. praise or smiles. Frequently teachers and parents get locked into an intensifying cycle of negative criticism which exacerbates the problem. Adolescents feel they can do nothing right and as a result cease to bother about improving their behaviour.

The parent or teacher must avoid inadvertently rewarding or reinforcing inappropriate behaviour.

If the teacher or parent feels that punishment is appropriate in the circumstances then to be effective it should meet the following criteria:

- It should not be such that it could be interpreted as physical or emotional abuse.
- It should punish the specific behaviour.
- It should occur as soon as possible after the misbehaviour.
- It should be proportionate to the misbehaviour.
- It should be consistently applied.
- It should produce the desired effect, i.e. a reduction or complete extinction of the misbehaviour.
- It should be coupled with reinforcers or rewards for appropriate behaviour.

For the behavioural approach to be effective it must be consistently applied over a period of time.

In practical terms, teachers and parents should remember what the adolescent's behaviour was like in order to identify increases or trends in positive behaviour.

Derivable from the assessment there should be a formulation which is a statement as to why the behaviour is occurring and how it is being maintained. This formulation has the status of a testable hypothesis which should lead to an appropriate intervention.

Cognitive-behavioural approach

Basic assumptions of the cognitive-behavioural approach:

- Negative cognitions are associated with emotional and behavioural difficulties.
- One's attentional and retrieval biases operate in a way that selects negative information, so helping to maintain problems.
- Meta-cognition, i.e. one's particular thinking about one's own cognitive processes, can exacerbate problems.
- Negative cognitions can be changed by logical challenges or by arranging contrary experiences.

This approach is based on the idea that an adolescent's emotional and behavioural difficulties are mainly the product of maladaptive cognitive processes.

The phrase **cognitive processes** refers to the following: thoughts, beliefs, expectations, attitudes and attributions.

In reaction to behaviourism, the cognitive approach emphasises that it is necessary to consider the contribution made to an individual's emotional and behavioural difficulties by his or her cognitive processes. An adolescent's thought processes can lead to him or her behaving appropriately or inappropriately. Interventions are directed at changing or altering cognitive processes that in turn affect behaviour positively.

There are various forms of **cognitive intervention** including:

- **Ellis's (1990) rational-emotive therapy**
- **Beck's (1976) cognitive therapy**
- **Meichenbaum's (1977) self-instructional training**
- **D'Zurilla's (1986) problem-solving therapy**
- **Bandura's (1977) social learning approach.**

All of the above are cognitive interventions that aim at restructuring an individual's maladaptive thought processes as a way of increasing appropriate behaviour.

Rational-emotive behaviour therapy (REBT) (Ellis, 1990)

The fundamental assumptions of REBT are that:

- Individuals' beliefs influence their thinking, feelings and behaviour about themselves, other people and their environment.

- Some beliefs lead to positive feelings and behaviour; others lead to negative feelings and behaviour.

- It is possible to identify negative beliefs and to modify them.

- People who subscribe to a number of absolute 'musts' end up irrationally believing that unless things are perfect then they will not be able to achieve their goals.

> The therapy consists of:
>
> - questioning and challenging irrational beliefs from a scientific standpoint, a process called **Disputing Irrational Beliefs**, i.e. understanding the illogical, non-empirical and non-pragmatic consequences of holding such beliefs;
>
> - didactic instruction, i.e. showing why these beliefs are irrational;
>
> - providing homework assignments that help the individual to avoid dependency on the therapist and also prolong the therapeutic sessions;
>
> - enabling the person to move from a purely intellectual insight into his or her irrational beliefs to an emotional insight, i.e. a desire to change those beliefs.

This approach therefore sees emotional and behavioural difficulties as resulting from irrational self-statements that adolescents make about themselves. An **ABC analysis** is used to describe a sequence of events which result in the continuation of maladaptive behaviour.

A refers to the antecedent event that triggers the problem, **B** stands for the adolescent's irrational belief about the preceding event and **C** is the consequence of that irrational belief.

As an example, an adolescent girl is rejected by her boyfriend, antecedent event (A); this leads her to the irrational belief that she is unattractive and that no other boys will ever like her again, event (B), and as a consequence becomes depressed, event (C).

The intervention to remedy this problem of depression proceeds as follows: first, the event that precipitates the girl's irrational belief is identified and clarified; second, the specific negative self-statements the girl makes are also identified along with the underlying irrational beliefs; and finally, the girl is helped to challenge those irrational self-statements through a process of analysis, disputation and substitution of positive for negative self-statements.

Cognitive therapy (CT) (Beck, 1976)

The fundamental assumptions of CT are that:

- Individuals make **cognitive appraisals** of themselves, other people and their environments.

- People have their own **schemas** which comprise a set of organising principles and core beliefs that structure perceptions of themselves and their environment, e.g. latent **depressogenic schemas** structure experience in terms of loss or worthlessness; **cognitive distortions** operate that maintain these schemas through the biased selection of information and as a result produce **cognitive deficits**, i.e. the lack of normal cognitive processing.

- Individuals experience **automatic thoughts** that seem to arise unconsciously at times of stress.

The therapy consists of:

- actively encouraging people themselves to find supporting or conflicting evidence for their interpretations, to look for alternative explanations and to undertake different courses of action based on these explanations (**collaborative empiricism**);

- enabling people to set goals, undertake homework tasks and provide feedback;

- engaging in a **Socratic dialogue** with people to tease out the logical and empirical consequences of their particular thoughts and behaviours (**guided discovery**).

A theory of depression

People who experience depression possess a particular negative cognitive schema which is activated by stressful events; this activation results in people having feelings of sadness, worthlessness and hopelessness. This depressogenic schema has a bias for negative information and also screens out positive information that would fail to maintain the schema. The schema is not the cause, which can be due to a range of factors, but is rather a means by which the depression develops.

In connection with this theory, certain common cognitive distortions have been identified:

- **arbitrary inference**: basing one's beliefs on insufficient evidence while ruling out competing interpretations;

- **selective abstraction**: basing one's beliefs on selected evidence while ignoring conflicting evidence;

- **over-generalisation**: basing one's beliefs on the generalisation from a few instances;

- **magnification or minimisation**: basing one's beliefs on the exaggeration or the devaluing of the significance of one event.

This approach, therefore, sees adolescents' emotional and behavioural difficulties as arising from negative schemas that are triggered by stressful events. Observable behaviour can be traced to the operation of a particular negative schema.

Adolescents are asked for their perceptions and explanations of their problems and these are then explored particularly in terms of misconceptions or cognitive distortions. Core beliefs and attitudes are established; in particular, those that are expressive of self-efficacy and those that relate to causal attributions. Adolescents are asked to engage in self-monitoring, i.e. to identify those thoughts, especially automatic thoughts, that are associated with their particular problems. They are asked to write these down. Finally, they are asked to see if they can arrive at alternative beliefs or explanations and to subject these to empirical tests.

Self-instructional training (Meichenbaum, 1977)

This approach is based on Ellis's rational-emotive theory that children develop control over their behaviour through internal speech and symbolic control. This approach incorporates both **cognitive modelling** and **cognitive-behavioural rehearsal**.

This form of training requires an appropriate role model to model specific, positive self-statements which the adolescent then in turn models and rehearses. Self-instructional training can be enhanced by using imagery manipulation and relaxation techniques.

Problem-solving training (D'Zurilla, 1986)

Emotional and behavioural difficulties are seen as resulting from internal and/or external demands or needs that exceed the coping skills the individual has in his or her repertoire. A solution is provided by equipping the individual with the necessary coping skills to deal with the problems.

The problem-solving model consists of five components:

- **The stage of problem orientation**:

problem perception	recognising and labelling the problem;
problem attribution	refers to what an individual attributes his or her problem to, e.g. personal or environmental factors;
problem appraisal	a person's evaluation of the significance of the problem for him or her;
personal control	the likelihood that a person sees a problem as controllable and that he or she has the power to solve that problem;
Personal time and effort	the likelihood that a person thinks he or she has sufficient time and commitment to solve the problem.

- **The stage of problem-definition and formulation**: the problem should be defined in clear, specific and concrete terms, goals should be set and the problem stated in terms of possible alternative formulations, i.e. reasons why it occurs and why it continues.

- **The stage of the generation of alternative solutions**: alternative solutions should be generated in terms of both quantity and variety.

- **The stage of decision-making**: the aim is to compare and judge which of the alternative solutions is the optimal one in terms of the costs and benefits of each solution.

- **The stage of solution implementation and verification**: the aim is to implement a particular solution and judge its effectiveness in real-life situations; it is necessary to avoid unrealistic goals and performance indicators.

Social learning approach (Bandura, 1977)

This approach is based on the theory of **reciprocal determinism** which is that a person's behaviour can influence his or her environment, as well as the environment influencing a person's behaviour. People through their cognitive processes are in a position to discriminate between different situations and as a result their behaviour can come to depend on the specific situation they find themselves in and it can also vary across contexts.

The main components of the social learning approach are:

perceived self-efficacy	which is a person's perceived ability to deal with a current problem, task or situation. Self-efficacy arises through actual achievement, vicarious experiences of seeing others achieve, persuasion and emotional arousal.
observational learning	which is a person's ability to learn new behaviours by observing others, those others being people modelling the behaviours. Physical and verbal aggression can be learned through adolescents observing the aggressive behaviour of others, e.g. family members and peers and through aggression depicted in films.
self-regulation	which is a person's ability to control his or her own behaviour, expectancies or anticipated consequences, there being two types of expectancies – outcome expectations, that a particular behaviour will produce a certain result, and efficacy expectations, that one will be able to perform that behaviour.
self-reinforcement	where people reward themselves for achieving their goals.

Adolescent emotional and behavioural difficulties can arise through a process of learning, i.e. learning maladaptive behavioural and emotional responses through observing models, e.g. parents and peers. Negative expectations and feelings of inefficacy can also play a part in helping to produce emotional and behavioural problems. This occurs where adolescents think that they do not have the ability or resources to influence events in their lives. Anxiety results from perceived inefficacy in coping with potential or actual problems and from the negative expectation that painful consequences will ensue unless anxiety-evoking situations are avoided.

The social learning approach treats emotional and behavioural difficulties through a process of **modelling** and **guided participation**.

Modelling is where a competent individual or model demonstrates appropriate behaviour to the adolescent and guided participation is where the model helps the adolescent to perform the appropriate behaviour. Modelling can help adolescents to acquire new behaviours and coping skills.

The cognitive approach for teachers and parents

Teachers and parents should be aware that sometimes adolescents hold irrational, illogical and distorted beliefs, attitudes and expectations about themselves and others. They may be prone to think unduly negatively about their abilities, their attractiveness and their future prospects particularly in comparison to their peers.

Teachers and parents should help adolescents to identify and correct irrational and illogical thinking about themselves and others, e.g. where adolescents make sweeping generalisations, where they make unfounded assertions and where they exaggerate or underestimate their own abilities or attractiveness. Similarly, teachers and parents should engage in this exercise themselves with respect to their own thinking processes about adolescents.

Teachers and parents should encourage adolescents to identify and focus on positive aspects of themselves and ask them to make positive self-statements about themselves.

Solution-focused brief therapy (SFBT) approach

The solution-focused brief therapy (SFBT) approach is a type that has its origin in family therapy, particularly that of de Shazer (1985) and has as its underlying basis **social constructionism**. The brief in brief therapy usually means fewer than 20 sessions. The brevity of the therapy is aimed at avoiding dependency and loss of clarity and focus over time.

The main elements of brief therapy include:

- identifying current problems and specifying achievable goals clearly and quickly;
- focusing on the present;
- seeing people as having problems, not being problems;
- minimal intervention in people's lives;
- focusing on strengths and resources the person already possesses;
- developing and evaluating action plans in collaboration with the person.

This approach has been applied to a range of problems including psychiatric illness, alcoholism, sexual abuse, parenting and school difficulties. It has been used in different settings including educational (school and college), health and social services.

The SFBT approach asks certain specific questions:

- How will you know if it has been successful and how can it be helpful?
- Focusing on specifics, what do you wish to change?
- Have we clarified the problems and are there occasions when these problems do not arise?
- What will life be like without these problems?
- What competencies and resources does the person possess?
- What form of reciprocal collaboration will there be?
- Has it been successful enough for the therapy to be terminated?

The result of these questions will be a contract. This contract will establish the basis for collaborative work but will not predetermine the number and frequency of the sessions.

The principles that guide the work are:

- The person does not need to be cured but is temporarily unable to cope with a problem.
- There should be a period of problem-free conversation in order to build up a profile of the person's strengths and resources.
- The focus is on a process of change which is seen as gradual and incremental.
- Talk focuses on people's competencies or coping strategies past and present that have succeeded or failed and on exceptions or when problems do not occur.
- Problems are reframed or put in a different context in order to make them more amenable to solution.
- Solution talk focuses on providing support and encouragement, on asking the person in what ways life will be different once the problem is solved or is made more manageable (the **miracle question**), on asking the person to scale

from 10 to zero where he or she is now in terms of the problem (the **scaling question**) and by asking the person to look at the problem from a different perspective (the **reframing question**).

● Talk about strategies includes enlisting the skills and resources of the person in order to realise that person's goals, ways of achieving those goals and ways of evaluating progress.

This approach requires the therapist in the first session to do the following:

● be attentive and focus on change;
● show empathy and respect;
● be collaborative;
● acknowledge effort and progress;
● ask questions that facilitate change by opening up different possibilities and perspectives;
● use language that avoids labelling;
● help set clear, specific, positive, incremental and achievable goals;
● ask the miracle question to clarify goals and ways they can be realised;
● consider failed solutions so lessons can be learned;
● find out the person's strengths and resources and perhaps set a task.

Other sessions require the therapist:

● to assess change and to ask what is working through scaling questions;
● to enable the person to report failure as well as progress with respect to tasks;
● to ask the client to make predictions as to what will happen if change is perceived as random and non-repeatable;
● to reinforce the person's strategies;
● to reframe the problem, looking at alternatives, and externalise it by looking at the problem together as external and test problems by challenging the person's views of them;
● to use scaling questions to determine that sufficient progress has been achieved and that the therapy should end.

The SFBT approach

This approach has been used with children, adolescents and parents. With adolescents it is important to establish a collaborative relationship at the outset. It is also necessary to select the 'right' problem, define the problem clearly and, specifically, listen to adolescents' accounts or narratives, give them a 'voice' and utilise their strengths and resources in order to generate solutions.

It is useful to collect information on the adolescent's self-motivation, social and problem-solving skills and school or college functioning.

The adolescent is then asked what his or her goals and desired outcomes should be. The miracle question can be used in this respect. Scaling questions can also be used to enable the adolescent to state where the problem is on a scale 10 to zero and where the adolescent would like to be in an agreed period of time. It is helpful to externalise the problem where adolescents feel or have been told that their problems are internal. Externalising the problem helps overcome passivity and defensiveness arising from a sense of past failure.

Certain tasks can facilitate change where identifying exceptions to problems has not occurred, e.g. **Prediction tasks** where change is seen as random and unintentional, **Do Something Different tasks** where change is not forthcoming and **Pretend the Miracle** has occurred where change is not seen as significant. Adolescents and parents should be encouraged not to see setbacks as failures but as a normal part of the change process. As regards parenting, parents need to set aside a special time for their adolescent daughters and sons to enable them to feel valued and nurtured. Surprising their adolescent children by acting differently than they normally do can help surmount or circumvent negative adolescent–parent relationships. Another strategy is to use positive consequences; this is where an adolescent is asked to perform a positive task rather than a sanction in order to make amends for misbehaviour.

Person-centred (Rogerian) approach

This approach has as its main focus the individual's reflective self-awareness or subjective experience. It assumes a **phenomenological standpoint** where individuals are seen as acting according to their subjective awareness of themselves and their world. Respect for this individuality of awareness and experience is seen as fundamental. From this viewpoint the aim of teachers and parents should be to encourage adolescents to discover and explore their inner resources so that they will be able to fulfil their potential and cope with the challenges posed by adolescence.

People are seen as possessing an inherent **actualising tendency** which means that they strive to grow and realise their full potential. There is an emphasis on people's perceptions, feelings, subjectivity, self-actualisation and the whole process of change. Self-actualisation is a process of change whereby the self moves from simplicity to complexity, from dependency to autonomy and from rigidity of thought to free expression. Emphasis is on individual creative development or growth.

As individuals grow or develop, particular needs arise. An individual has a need for **positive regard** and also **self-regard**. Positive regard includes warmth, respect, sympathy and acceptance. Experiencing self-regard depends on positive regard shown by others. If the positive regard of others has been selective or conditional, then **conditions of worth** become operative. Self-regard becomes dependent solely on meeting the demands and wishes of others. Individuals who have become preoccupied with meeting conditions of worth will not possess self-confidence in decision-making and are said to be lacking an internalised locus of evaluation. Those who experience a lack of positive regard and self-regard are at risk of developing emotional problems.

The **self** is a fundamental concept in this approach. The individual interprets as well as perceives the external world. The self is composed of organised perceptions and the meanings attached to those perceptions. This is the **actual self**.

The **ideal self** is that self which the individual would most like to be and includes those perceptions and meanings that he or she would most like to experience. This self is primarily a conscious one although there are experiences which the self has but of which it is unaware. Individuals may undergo **incongruency** between what they perceive as their self and their experiences. Anxiety can arise when they experience this incongruency. Generally, individuals are aware of their experiences but sometimes, through a process called **subception,** they may stop being aware of their experiences. A threatening experience may be registered as in conflict with the individual's self-concept and be suppressed but, in being suppressed, evokes anxiety. The individual will attempt to maintain self-integrity by the use of defences, i.e. through **distortion**, the experience being transformed into one consistent with the self and through **denial**, preventing the experience entering awareness.

A **fully functioning** person is one who is realistic, who is open to experience, who trusts experience, who evaluates experience and adjusts or adapts accordingly, i.e. who is prepared to change and grow.

When individuals experience emotional problems, therapeutic change is facilitated by three core conditions:

- congruence or genuineness
- acceptance or unconditional positive regard
- empathy

Parent–child relationships are conducive to growth where parents are democratic and provide positive appraisals of their children. Children who experience low self-esteem are those who have generally received a punitive upbringing based on the use of punishment and the withdrawal of love or an upbringing where parents did not establish and enforce boundaries.

Psychodynamic approach

There are quite a few psychodynamic approaches to emotional and behavioural difficulties; all originate in Freudian psychoanalysis. These approaches are based on the following assumptions:

- that an individual's internal world of drives, desires, object representations and associated conflicts are manifested in different types of emotional and behavioural problems;
- that these conflicts have their origin in early childhood;

- that these conflicts are often **unconscious**, i.e. there is no conscious awareness of them and they are inaccessible except under special conditions;

- that unconscious conflicts may appear in **symbolic** or **metaphorical** forms in dreams, in the symptoms of stress or in the effects of substance abuse;

- that unconscious conflicts cause anxiety or psychological pain, the intensity of which evokes a variety of defences or defence mechanisms against that pain.

Freudian psychoanalysis

Freudian psychoanalysis emphasises sexual and aggressive drives which need to be controlled and redirected and sees an individual's **psychosexual development** as proceeding through stages, i.e. oral, anal, phallic-Oedipal, latency and puberty. If individuals do not proceed through these stages satisfactorily, they become **fixated** at a particular stage and resort to infantile behaviour or at stressful times **regress** to such behaviour. An individual also needs to resolve his or her **Oedipus complex** which is where that individual has sexual feelings for the parent of the opposite sex and wants to exclude the parent of the same sex. The complex is resolved through **identification** with the parent of the same sex and temporary exclusion of the parent of the opposite sex.

Freud developed a **structural model of the mind** composed of the concepts of **id**, **ego** and **superego**.

The id is the biological source of our sexual and aggressive drives and these drives seek expression without hindrance or constraint. The id therefore observes the pleasure principle, desiring immediate gratification in either fantasy or reality. It operates illogically, irrationally and egocentrically.

The ego observes the reality principle, utilising logic and reason. It attempts to guide the urgent drives of the id into acceptable channels, it is orientated towards the future and so tolerates frustration and delays gratification in order to achieve its aims.

The superego is our conscience which is the source of our moral values and ideals and acts to control our behaviour in accordance with those values and ideals. It is composed of the internalised representations and values of our parents. At times it can be over-strict, making us feel guilty without reason and it can also be simplistic, ignoring the nuances of a problem, and perfectionist, striving to reach unrealistic ideals.

An individual can experience acute anxiety or psychological pain arising from unconscious conflicts, particularly unconscious sexual and aggressive desires that come into conflict with the superego's moral strictures.

Unconscious processes

Dreams are seen as a route into the unconscious and are described as having a **manifest** or reported content and a **latent** or interpreted content that reveals the workings of the unconscious and its conflicts. They express **wish-fulfilment** and are also a way in which conflicts can be resolved. By the process of interpretation it is possible to understand the meaning of the symbolism that appears in the dream. The symbolism of the dream reveals the nature of unconscious conflicts.

Parapraxes are slips of the tongue or pen which arise due to unconscious conflicts and which through interpretation can reveal the nature of those conflicts.

Defence mechanisms

Anxiety or pain is controlled or prevented from surfacing through **defences**, e.g.:

projection	Our aggressive impulses are externalised (projected) onto others and seen as their aggressive behaviour towards us.
denial	We deny that we are displaying aggressive impulses even when we are being overtly hostile to others.
isolation	We think or fantasise aggressive acts but without any associated hostile feelings, i.e. there is an emphasis on rational thought at the expense of feelings.
intellectualisation	We analyse our aggressive impulses as if they were simply abstract or intellectual problems without any associated emotions.
undoing	We undo an irresistible impulse to perform an aggressive act by replacing it with an acceptable act, e.g. a religious ritual.
reaction formation	We deal with an aggressive impulse, e.g. a desire to inflict pain and injury by expressing its extreme opposite, pacifism.
rationalisation	We explain away our selfish, aggressive behaviour as reasonable assertion of our rights.
repression	Our aggressive impulses are kept unconscious.
sublimation	Our aggressive impulses are directed into cultural outlets.

Relationships

Transference is where intense feelings, e.g. of dependency, jealousy, hatred and frustration experienced in past relationships, e.g. with parents and siblings, are transferred to other people in the present. It can be seen also as representing infantile desires for achieving gratification through current relationships. Transference can be positive (feelings are positive) or negative (feelings are negative). Transference can also occur in relation to institutions as can counter-transference.

Relationships between a student and a teacher can be transferential in that the student may transfer positive or negative feelings towards their teacher as though his or her teacher were their parent.

Counter-transference is where, for example, teachers experience intense feelings evoked by their students' behaviour. It can be positive or negative. Where students come for advice to teachers, teachers may feel inadequate or guilty in not being able to help the student. They may see themselves as rescuing the child or being a parent substitute. Teachers may also find that conflicts they experienced in adolescence may re-emerge, triggered by their students' conflicts. They may act out their own feelings through vicarious identification with those of their students. For a teacher the counter-transference can be a source of information in terms of the effect of the student on others.

Phantasies

Phantasies must be distinguished from fantasies. Phantasies are unconscious fantasies, i.e. unconscious thoughts or feelings whereas fantasies are conscious thoughts or feelings. Phantasies influence our thoughts, perceptions, feelings and behaviour. We may have phantasies of putting parts of our inner world into others, e.g. expelling unpleasant feelings or taking parts of others into our inner world, e.g. their qualities or attributes. Life events and evoked memories of those events might trigger particular phantasies, e.g. the death of a parent might unleash feelings of guilt.

In relation to children or students with emotional and behavioural difficulties, teachers may have particular phantasies, e.g.:

- A teacher may unconsciously collude with pupils or students in their oppositional behaviour to authority due to conflicts the teacher had with their own parents in the past.
- Teachers may unconsciously idealise themselves, seeing themselves as better 'parents' than the parents of their pupils or students.
- Teachers may unconsciously idealise their pupils or students, seeing them as better than others.
- Teachers faced with extreme aggressiveness in pupils or students may unconsciously feel an equally aggressive and punitive reaction towards them.
- Teachers may have unconscious feelings that they are able magically to cure or rescue their pupils or students from their difficulties.

Projective techniques

Projective techniques are designed to reveal the symbolic and metaphorical meanings and the feelings which inhabit the unconscious of individuals. Such techniques require the presentation to individuals of ambiguous stimuli which individuals then respond to according to the nature of their unconscious conflicts.

Examples of projective techniques are the following:

inkblot test (Rorshach)	Ten cards with ambiguous inkblots on them. Interpretation of responses is made on the basis of all the responses. The idea is that an individual's responses will be determined by the ways in which their unconscious conflicts will structure and organise their perceptions of the inkblots.
thematic apperception test (Morgan and Murray)	This is composed of cards that depict ambiguous scenes. On the basis of these scenes the individual is asked to invent a story. The type of story recounted is seen as being determined by the individual's unconscious conflicts.
free association	This process occurs where individuals observe the basic rule, i.e. articulate their thoughts fully without attempting to censor or impede them. The aim is to circumvent resistances which may prevent unconscious conflicts coming into conscious awareness.

Interpretation

Interpretation is the process through which the unconscious is made conscious and conflicts are brought to the surface, enabling the individual to gain insight into those conflicts. This is achieved by overcoming the resistances and defences which are barriers to interpretation. Interpretation requires the understanding of symbolic and metaphorical meanings, e.g. of an individual's dreams, language, communication and behaviour. The aim of interpretation is to enable individuals to become aware of their unconscious conflicts and thereby resolve them.

Bowlby's psychodynamic theory

Bowlby's central concept is that of **attachment** where an individual is emotionally dependent on another, usually older individual. Evidence for such an attachment is indicated by an individual seeking proximity, needing a secure base and feeling anxiety if the attachment is lost or threatened.

There are various forms of attachment:

- **secure type**: where the individual has a secure base from which to explore his or her environment and which provides a strong foundation for future psychological development;

● **insecure type**: where the individual avoids the care-provider or displays ambivalence or rejection towards the care-giver and as a result finds relationships difficult.

Proximity-seeking behaviour occurs so that a **secure base** can be established that enables that individual to explore his or her environment without fear or anxiety. If individuals lack a secure base, then they may end up feeling defensive rather than self-confident and as a result engage in destructive behaviours, e.g. becoming aggressive, in an attempt to minimise separation anxiety.

With regard to adolescents, they tend to attach and reattach themselves to parents or carers and eventually detach themselves from their parents or care-provider through the medium of their peer group on the way to adulthood. Adolescents may at times appear to be rejecting their parents but, when faced with stress, return for support from their parents. They are simply expressing their desire to form their own identity by reacting against their parents while wishing to retain a secure base if they find themselves in trouble. Parental acknowledgement of this process may help them to avoid experiencing unnecessary conflicts with their adolescent children.

If adolescents experience threatened or actual loss or a bereavement in childhood, this often assumes the form of a separation anxiety which if not adequately coped with can result in relationship problems with peers or psychiatric problems in adult life, e.g. depression and phobic behaviour. Adolescents can also be adversely emotionally affected by various environmental traumas, e.g. disruption or cessation of caring, threats of separation or suicide by parents, being told they are unwanted by their parents or that they are the wrong sex. Rejected children whether rejected by parents or their peers tend to think of themselves negatively. Children rejected because of their aggression tend to develop the following sort of problems in adolescence: conduct disorders, truancy, low educational achievement, exclusion from school and juvenile delinquency. Children rejected because they are socially withdrawn tend to become fearful and anxious.

Ecosystemic approach

The ecosystemic approach is based on systems theory which emphasises interactions within and between systems. The focus is not only on individuals and their personal characteristics but also the relationships between individuals and other individuals, and those individuals and the systems in which they are embedded. A person's beliefs and actions not only influence his or her environment but the environment also influences that person's beliefs and actions.

The origin of this approach can be traced to von Bertalanffy (1968) and Bateson (1979) and also to the work of family therapists such as Minuchin (Structural approach, 1974) and Molnar and de Shazer (Strategic therapy, 1985).

General systems theory

The main elements of general systems theory are:

systems	focus on patterns of relationships within or between systems, e.g. families are more than simply the sum of their individual members;
suprasystems	systems and subsystems are themselves embedded in an all-encompassing suprasystem;
open system	focus on systems open to external influences, e.g. families are open systems;
closed system	focus on systems sealed off from external influences;
subsystems	focus on parts of the system and their functions within the system as a whole, e.g. the roles that family members play in the family;
boundaries	focus on boundaries between individuals, subsystems and systems, e.g. with families, boundaries are semi-permeable;
homeostasis	focus on the preservation of stability or equilibrium of a system or family;
organisation	focus on the whole system or family as an inter-relationship of parts;
rules	focus on the rules of an organisation, system or family;
cybernetics and feedback loops (positive and negative)	focus on self-regulation of a system or family through feedback.

The aim is to change negative interactional patterns of behaviour for positive ones. Thus, the focus is on changing the family as a whole rather than one individual.

Ecosystemic approach to emotional and behavioural difficulties

Emotional and behavioural difficulties are seen as resulting from negative interactions between individuals and other subsystems, e.g. siblings and parents or between subsystems; parents and other systems; schools and the local community.

Negative interactions may arise due to misperceptions or misconceptions held by individuals about themselves and about each other. These negative interactions may increase as a result of these misconceptions feeding on each other.

Emotional and behavioural difficulties are therefore seen as:

- resulting from social interactions, not simply as being problems within individuals (an interactionist analysis being favoured rather than a purely within-person analysis). Thus, parents and adolescents both contribute to the difficulties an adolescent experiences. Parental attitudes and actions can exacerbate pre-existing adolescent problems or even produce them.

- resulting from complex interactions between adolescents and wider systems and subsystems, e.g. between adolescents and college or school and between adolescents and siblings or peers.

- resulting from cyclical chains of actions and responses to those actions. From adolescents' standpoint their behaviour appears as a rational response to, say, a particular parental action or response to their behaviour. From a parental or teacher viewpoint, a particular adolescent action or response may appear problematic but for the adolescent it is a solution to a problem. Parental or teacher resistance can be seen as exacerbating the adolescent's problem. Teachers, parents and adolescents become locked into a self-perpetuating cycle of negative interactions.

- amenable to reflective analysis where parties to a conflict analyse their own behaviour and how it is contributing to the difficulties. Parents and teachers should analyse their attitudes, actions and responses to see how they might be contributing to adolescent problems. The aim is to avoid confrontational approaches and to seek co-operation with the adolescent. Parents and teachers should strive along with the adolescent to arrive at the meaning of the adolescent's behaviour and not dismiss it as 'mindless' or incomprehensible. One method of interpretation is that of 'reframing' where a parent or teacher puts a positive skew on what on the surface appears to be purely negative behaviour, e.g. an adolescent who engages in defiant behaviour such as wearing 'outrageous' clothes, coming home very late and leaving his or her room untidy may be seen as attempting to establish his or her own personal identity. This interpretation of the adolescent's behaviour is one that could be seen as plausible by all parties. The parental intervention could recognise that the adolescent's behaviour is positive in that the adolescent is striving to become autonomous but that it is excessive in relation to achieving that goal.

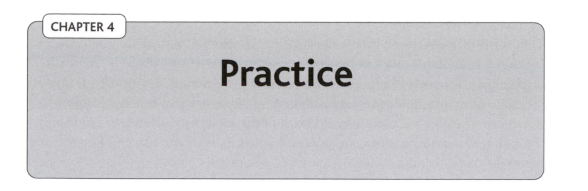

CHAPTER 4

Practice

Behavioural difficulties

The concept

Behavioural difficulties: these are best defined in terms of overt, observable and specific behaviours that are perceived as problems by the person experiencing them and/or by others perceiving/experiencing them as such.

Behavioural difficulties need to be seen within a developmental, cultural and normative context.

- Are the difficulties 'normal' for the developmental stage?
- Are the difficulties ones that pertain to all or most of the individuals in the reference group?
- Are the difficulties related to differences between cultures?

Types

Behavioural difficulties can be described in non-technical and technical terms.

In non-technical terms: **physical and verbal aggression, truancy**

In technical terms: **DSM-IV: attention-deficit hyperactivity disorder (ADHD), conduct disorder**

Behavioural approach

This approach is based on learning theory and explains behaviour difficulties as being the result of adolescents learning inappropriate behaviours or failing to learn appropriate behaviours. The behavioural approach has been used to treat severe mental disorders, e.g. autism and ADHD in conjunction with other approaches.

Behavioural assessment

This form of assessment focuses on overt, specific and observable behaviours. Inference is kept at a low level to avoid unsubstantiated speculation. The teacher or parent/carer needs to observe and record the problem behaviours in terms of latency, frequency, duration and intensity. Various assessment instruments or forms are available for observing and recording behaviour. The idea is to sample the behaviour and by doing so to detect patterns or trends in the behaviours emitted.

In particular it is useful to observe the antecedents and consequences of a given problem behaviour – an **ABC analysis**. This involves identifying incidents or events that trigger the problem behaviours and also the consequences of those problem behaviours.

The adolescent's behaviour should be observed where possible in different contexts, e.g. home, school, college and across different groups and situations. This is necessary in order to see whether the problem behaviour varies according to different contexts.

Ideally it is necessary to establish a pre-intervention baseline of the behaviours. This involves recording the latency, frequency, duration and intensity of the behaviours over a period of, say, two or three weeks. This baseline enables a comparison to be made between the start and end of an intervention. An intervention can then be evaluated in terms of whether an improvement in behaviour has occurred or not.

However, it may only be practicable for those responsible for planning and implementing an intervention to remember the behaviour at the start of the intervention and compare it with the behaviour at the end.

Behavioural formulation

This type of formulation is based on the premise that behaviour difficulties result from learning processes, i.e. operant conditioning. One looks for what reinforces and maintains a given adolescent's behavioural difficulties.

Behaviour difficulties are produced as a result of adolescents learning inappropriate behaviours (learning negative behaviours, e.g. using physical aggression to solve problems) or failing to learn appropriate behaviour in the first place (e.g. acquiring and employing assertiveness skills instead of physical aggression to solve problems).

Behavioural intervention

These interventions are based on primarily using positive reinforcement, negative reinforcement, extinction and punishment to modify behaviour.

- **Positive reinforcement** is where a behaviour occurring prior to the employment of a positive reinforcer increases, e.g. an adolescent who helps his or her parent or works hard for a teacher is rewarded by praise or privileges and this has the effect of increasing those desired behaviours.

- **Negative reinforcement:** when negative reinforcers are presented, the behaviour occurring prior to the employment of the negative reinforcers decreases or ends. The behaviours increase when a negative reinforcer is removed, e.g. a parent shouting at an adolescent to tidy up his or her bedroom. The negative reinforcer is the act of shouting as it leads the adolescent to tidy up the room; thus, the adolescent learns to tidy up the room to avoid his or her parent's ire.

- **Extinction** is where positive reinforcement is removed, e.g. a teacher stops paying attention to a student shouting out for help, the teacher only taking heed of the student's request if quietly asked. As a result, the student stops shouting out and is increasingly polite. This technique is best combined with positive reinforcement of appropriate behaviour.

- **Punishment** is where a positive reinforcer is taken away or where sanctions are inflicted when an offence is committed. Privileges can be withdrawn, e.g. a parent stops an adolescent son from watching a favourite late night TV show, or uses sanctions like grounding him for coming home late.

Behavioural evaluation

This form of evaluation is based on observing the beginning and end of an intervention through a process of reassessment. The behaviour at the end of an intervention is compared with the baseline intervention in order to establish whether positive behavioural change has occurred.

It should be noted that although positive behavioural change may have occurred statistically, the change or degree of change may not be deemed sufficient for those involved to consider the intervention effective. This is the difference between statistical and clinical significance.

Parents and behavioural difficulties

Parental styles:

In the first instance parents are advised to adopt an authoritative style of parenting and avoid authoritarian or laissez-faire styles.

- An **authoritative** style is one where parents are firm and warm towards their children and also use discussion and reasoning to resolve conflicts.

- An **authoritarian** style is one where parents adopt a purely coercive or punitive approach, not discussing or reasoning with their children but simply punishing them.

- A **laissez-faire** style is one where parents do not provide supervision or guidance for their children but leave them to their own devices.

Behavioural techniques:

Parents should find it relatively easy to understand and implement a behavioural approach towards dealing with adolescent problems.

- Positive reinforcement should be used where adolescents present appropriate behaviour – this can take the form of praise, the restoration of privileges or the provision of rewards. It must be realised that inadvertently, inappropriate behaviour can also be positively reinforced.

- Positive reinforcement must be consistently applied and must be made conditional on appropriate behaviour. It should be recognised that behaviour will probably be need to be shaped, i.e. a series of approximations to the behaviour will need to be reinforced before the target behaviour is achieved. Rewards must be ones that adolescents themselves perceive as such and they must be sufficiently desirable to motivate them to change their behaviour. There may be variations in behaviour, i.e. peaks and troughs, and because of this there is a need to look out for upward or downward trends in behaviour across time.

It may be possible for parents to negotiate a contract with their adolescent sons/daughters, setting specific targets along with rewards for meeting those targets. The contract can be verbal or written as long as all concerned are committed and clearly understand what is involved.

Teachers and behavioural difficulties

Teachers, like parents, should find it relatively easy to introduce behavioural methods into their classrooms. The same conditions listed above apply to the classroom situation. Teachers sometimes find it difficult to develop a habit of praising or rewarding their students' behaviour, preferring to use punishment.

Cognitive-behavioural approach

This approach combines cognitive, social learning and behavioural perspectives. The cognitive approach encompasses cognitive processes, e.g. attitudes, expectations, attributions, beliefs and perceived self-efficacy.

Cognitive-behavioural assessment

This type of assessment combines behavioural with cognitive assessment:

- The behavioural component looks at the nature of the adolescent's specific and observable behaviour, its context, its consequences, its frequency, duration and the adolescent's observed interactions with others.
- The cognitive component complements behavioural assessment by including information on the adolescent's cognitive processes, i.e. thoughts and feelings, particularly those apparently relating to the adolescent's behavioural and emotional difficulties. This means, for example, recording beliefs, attitudes, motivation and attributions relevant to the difficulties. This can be achieved through interviews and self-reports. This involves identifying the specific cognitive processes that contribute to the problem and those that help to maintain it. This will include the adolescent's perceptions and the views of others involved with the adolescent, e.g. parents, relatives and peers.

Cognitive formulation

This type of formulation states how an adolescent's particular beliefs, attitudes, perceived self-efficacy and attributions lead to their behavioural difficulties.

Eight cognitive interventions

1. Self-management/Self-control: the aim is for adolescents to learn how environmental triggers influence their behaviour. Adolescents keep a record of those triggers that elicit certain behaviours, thoughts and feelings, e.g. through an ABC chart. They learn to eliminate or reduce the influence of negative cognitive processes, e.g. negative perceptions and irrational thoughts and beliefs.

Adolescents can learn to reinforce their own appropriate behaviours through self-rewarding on accomplishment of those behaviours.

2. Self-instructional training (Meichenbaum, 1977): the aim here is to concentrate on those internal dialogues, which help to maintain the adolescent's inappropriate behaviour. The intervention involves changing negative self-statements to positive ones. It also involves helping adolescents to develop coping skills.

3. Problem-solving training (D'Zurilla, 1986): the aim is to train the adolescent to develop and employ problem-solving skills. The problem-solving process develops in stages:

- problem perceptions: recognising and identifying the problem;
- problem attribution: attributing the problem to the actions of others or to the environment;
- problem appraisal: evaluating the significance of the problem for oneself;
- problem definition and formulation: clearly defining the problem;
- generating alternatives: looking at alternative solutions to the problem;
- solution implementation and verification: putting the solution into practice and assessing the effectiveness of the solution.

4. Stress-inoculation training (Meichenbaum, 1977): the aim here is to go through a sequence of coping skills that enable the adolescent to deal with stressful situations. Adolescents are required to practise or rehearse the appropriate skills.

5. Cognitive restructuring (Ellis, 1990): the aim is to change or replace an adolescent's particular cognitive style or way of thinking. Ellis has identified a number of irrational modes of thought that lead to behavioural problems. By enabling the adolescent to think logically, empirically and pragmatically, other alternative, adaptive behaviours are considered and practised.

6. Social learning (Bandura, 1977): the aim is to enable adolescents to acquire and maintain appropriate behaviour through observational learning and modelling. Parents and teachers through their own actions model behaviours they wish adolescents to imitate. Adolescents are encouraged to identify with appropriate role models. The aim is also to encourage adolescents to increase their perceived self-efficacy, i.e. the belief that they are able to cope when faced with problem situations.

7. Social skills training: this type of training is designed to equip adolescents with skills that will facilitate successful relationships with others.

- The acquisition of social skills can help adolescents to achieve their goals or help them behave appropriately in given situations. What is deemed appropriate behaviour may depend on the social and cultural context.

Inappropriate behaviour may be due to:

- adolescents not possessing the relevant social skills;
- adolescents possessing social skills but not knowing how to use them;
- adolescents possessing relevant social skills but choosing not to use them.

Social skills can be divided into different components:

- non-verbal, e.g. posture, gestures, eye contact, facial expressions;
- verbal, e.g. aspects of speech/voice, speech content, listening/conversational skills;
- interpreting emotions, e.g. facial expressions, posture, speech/voice aspects.

Social skills can be assessed through using direct observation, questionnaires, self-report, peer reports, interviews and tests.

Social skills can be taught through direct instruction, problem-solving, modelling, role play and rehearsal.

8. Assertiveness training: the aim of this form of training is to help individuals to stand up for their rights in an appropriate way without infringing the rights of others.

A behavioural type of assessment is undertaken which can include a behavioural interview, self-report, self-monitoring, behavioural observation and role play.

This training can take place individually or in groups; however, training in groups appears more effective.

The actual training can take the form of overt and covert modelling, coaching, behavioural rehearsal, feedback, cognitive restructuring and homework assignments.

- **Overt modelling** or **observational learning**, where a person demonstrates assertive behaviour, can enable an adolescent to acquire new, more effective and appropriate ways of achieving legitimate goals.
- **Covert modelling**, where the adolescent imagines another person manifesting assertive behaviour, can also be effective.
- **Behaviour rehearsal** is where the adolescent overtly practises assertive behaviour; this may be combined with the trainer providing explicit instructions.
- **Feedback** is where the trainer helps shape an adolescent's assertive behaviour through coaching and positive reinforcement and by encouraging the adolescent to self-reinforce assertive behaviour. Audiotaped and videotaped feedback is very useful.

- **Cognitive restructuring** encourages the adolescent to substitute positive self-statements for negative self-statements.

Assertiveness training can benefit adolescents who manifest aggressive behaviour, those who are non-assertive, those who are stressed, those who are school refusers and those displaying social withdrawal.

Psychodynamic approach

This approach is based on the idea that behavioural and emotional difficulties result from inner, unconscious conflicts that have their origin in childhood relationships with parents, particularly in an early relationship with the mother.

In psychodynamic approaches the poor quality of the mother–child relationship is often seen as being the origin of behavioural and emotional problems in adolescence and adulthood, as, for example, in Winnicott (1965).

There is also an emphasis on children having adequate and safe **attachments** as in Bowlby (1988), particularly secure attachments where the child is sure that parents will be present and caring in moments of danger or stress. From this secure base the child feels confident in exploring the environment. **Anxious attachment** is where the child has experienced uncertainty and becomes reluctant to leave the parent and as a result lacks confidence in exploring the world. **Anxious avoidant attachment** is where the child wants care from the parent but expects rejection; the child ends up wanting to avoid the parent but at the same time desires the parent's love – the final outcome is an angry child.

Where children experience discontinuity in care, absence of care or loss of a parent or carer, they may lack the basis for trusting relationships. Furthermore, if children find that love from their parents is purely conditional and that they are rejected because they manifest unacceptable impulses, then they may well displace these unacceptable impulses elsewhere or deny their existence. The child who experiences the loss of a positive relationship can develop behavioural difficulties which result from intense anger felt at the loss. These children need a trusting relationship which will stand the tests and demands placed on it by their negative behaviour.

Psychodynamic approaches for parents and teachers

From a psychodynamic perspective teachers and parents should consider the following points in dealing with adolescents who manifest emotional and behavioural difficulties.

Understanding such difficulties may be helped by seeing them as resulting from **unconscious inner conflicts, separations** or **loss of relationships** experienced in early childhood.

Various unconscious defences may manifest themselves in children, teachers and parents, e.g.

- **Splitting**: situations and people are divided up into either good or bad; they are either good or bad, not good and bad together. For example, this can lead to teachers blaming parents for adolescents' problems and denying that they themselves in any way contribute to their problem.

- **Denial**: feelings or actions are denied; adolescents sometimes deny they have any problems.

- **Projection**: unpleasant, unacceptable or even acceptable feelings are pushed out onto other people. Adolescents sometimes see teachers and parents as being unfair, unreasonable and uncaring, not themselves. Alternatively, they may see themselves as having no good points at all.

Teachers and parents can help adolescents to feel secure and safe by:

- listening to their anxieties and their side of the story, being sympathetic and showing empathy;

- providing a secure base;

- setting boundaries and having high expectations;

- encouraging independence and autonomy rather than dependency;

- containing stress and anxiety;

- showing disapproval of their behaviour, not of them as people;

- outlining the consequences of their actions for themselves and others.

Teachers and parents should avoid:

- denying that they have negative feelings about them but strive to prevent those feelings interfering in their relationships with them;

- over- or under-identifying with adolescents, i.e. trying to be as it were one of them; having their feelings or attitudes or treating them as completely different beings with whom one has nothing in common;

- becoming non-involved, rejecting them or placing sole responsibility for them onto others.

Solution-focused brief therapy (de Shazer, 1985)

SFBT (see also Chapter 3) is a cognitive-based approach to adolescent problems that helps to identify concerns, goals and possible solutions. This approach consists of a number of techniques that can be used in the interview situation.

- Establish a rapport with the adolescent through general conversation.

- Agree goals for each session.

- Ask the adolescent to imagine what would happen if the problem miraculously disappeared, e.g. how would others know that the problem had gone and what would be their reactions. The aim here is to encourage the adolescent to recognise the benefits that result from the problem disappearing.

- Look with the adolescent at occasions when the problem did not occur and the reasons for its non-occurrence.

- The adolescent is asked to scale the problems along a continuum from 1 to 10; 1 being when the problem is at its worst and 10 when it has disappeared. The adolescent's scaling can be used to ask questions, e.g. regarding aspects of the problem, and if there has been change to what has occurred to bring that change about.
- The adolescent is asked to describe any social networks he or she can draw on to help him or her.
- The adolescent can be asked about any coping strategies he or she uses.
- At the end of each session there should be a summary of what has been achieved and goals for future sessions need to be set.

Emotional difficulties

The concept

Emotional difficulties are best seen as internalising problems where the adolescent experiences and suffers emotional upsets. They may not be detected by others if, for example, emotional difficulties do not result in overt behavioural difficulties. For this reason withdrawn, depressed and anxious adolescents may not receive support from teachers or parents.

As with behaviour difficulties, one should consider whether any particular emotional difficulty is developmentally 'normal'. Emotional difficulties can be broken down into three components:

- **behavioural**, e.g. running away from a problem situation, at home or school;
- **cognitive**, e.g. having irrational thoughts about oneself or others, thinking one is physically unattractive or that one is disliked by one's peers;
- **physiological**, e.g. sweating, dizziness and palpitations associated with a panic attack.

Types

In non-technical terms, e.g. anxiety, phobias and depression. In technical terms, e.g. (DSM-IV) Separation Anxiety Disorder.

Phobias are persistent, irrational and excessive fears. They are relatively common and can be debilitating.

Children at various ages do develop common fears, e.g. fear of strangers, fear of separation from parents. Adolescents can experience common fears, e.g. looking foolish in the eyes of their peers, losing their friends and appearing physically unattractive.

School refusal

This form of anxiety occurs where adolescents refuse to go to school. They feel sick, appear frightened and experience anxiety when away from their parents. This anxiety may lead them to absent themselves from school at the first opportunity.

The main criteria are:

- great difficulty in going to school, leading to long absences;
- intense emotional upset, fearfulness, temper tantrums, complaints of feeling ill where facing school;
- remaining at home with parents' knowledge;
- absence of deviant activities, e.g. theft, lying and vandalism.

NB: Adolescents who refuse to go to school and who do not experience anxiety and who are anti-social are deemed a separate category and classified as truants.

Depression

Adolescents can experience depression in the form of depressed mood, low self-esteem, hopelessness, helplessness, insomnia, changes in weight, irritability and thoughts of suicide. Adolescents may have experienced an actual loss of a significant other or fantasise such a loss. Parents and teachers may be unaware of depression in adolescents and as a result it may go untreated. Adolescents may complain of wanting to leave home, of not being understood, of feeling inadequate and of being rejected.

With respect to depression, teachers and parents may find that adolescents experience difficulties in articulating or expressing their feelings. In addition adolescents may not be given the opportunity to express their feelings or be listened to and they may be faced with incomprehension.

Adolescent suicide and attempted suicide

Suicide is rare before the age of 12 years but increases in adolescence.

Adolescents who attempt suicide may have a history of family problems, e.g. family conflict, bereavement and serious illness. There may also be evidence of the loss of a close relationship, social isolation and withdrawn behaviour, e.g. running away, long periods of silence and depressed moods. The adolescent has an overwhelming feeling of hopelessness and a sense that his or her problems are insoluble. He or she also feels unwanted, worried about the future and feel ashamed.

On the part of adolescents, there can also be a desire to highlight how they feel, to get back at people or to get them to change their mind, to test people's feelings for them or to gain help.

Adolescents who go on to commit suicide usually show signs of depression and may also display substance abuse, difficulties in school and general behaviour difficulties. They may feel socially isolated and imitate others who show suicidal behaviour.

Problem: Anxiety and phobias

anxiety   Some adolescents experience a generalised anxiety, a persistent, excessive and uncontrollable worry about problems; others experience a panic reaction.

panic attacks   These generally begin to occur in late adolescence. Adolescents experience thoughts and feelings of panic which occur along with physiological reactions, e.g. sweating, giddiness, hyperventilation and palpitations. There is also a fear of public embarrassment and as a result an overwhelming desire to vacate the public place in which the attack occurs. Some attacks occur unpredictably, others occur in response to specific situations. They can be associated with agoraphobia – a fear of leaving home and experiencing an attack in a public place.

phobias   Some adolescents experience an intense, persistent and unrealistic fear of an object or situation, resulting in avoidance. These phobias often first appear between the ages of 11 and 17. There are specific phobias, e.g. of animals. There is also social phobia: a pervasive fear of public embarrassment, a fear of making mistakes and avoidance of participation in public events. This phobia can arise in some adolescents due to acute self-consciousness.

school phobia   This occurs where an adolescent experiences emotional upsets, e.g. fear, temper outbursts and feelings of illness (nausea, vomiting, pains and diarrhoea) when faced with school attendance. The adolescent experiences intense anxiety while at school. The behavioural approach sees school phobia as a learned maladaptive behaviour. There may well be home- and school-related factors, e.g. at home, separation anxiety arises from mother–child dependency and at school there can be difficulties relating to particular teachers, learning difficulties and peer conflict. Parents can be seen from this perspective as inadvertently providing positive reinforcement for staying at home by being overprotective towards their child. Schools can be seen also as not providing sufficient reinforcement to encourage the pupil to stay in school as well as being places where anxiety-provoking incidents occur that bring about the pupil's absence.

Behavioural interventions are based on classical and operant conditioning. Where there is severe anxiety, classical conditioning approaches have been used, e.g. imaginary and/or real-life systematic desensitisation and flooding. Operant techniques have been used, e.g. increasing reinforcement at school and reducing it at home.

Behavioural assessment

It is necessary to identify the actual responses to the feared stimuli. In terms of overt behaviour there is avoidance, in terms of physiology there are increases in heart rate and in terms of cognition there are negative expectations.

Use an **ABC analysis** – it is helpful to identify the antecedents that appear to elicit the response, e.g. a specific animal or a public requirement such as sitting an exam or doing PE. It is also useful to look at the consequences of the behaviour – what others do when the adolescent experiences fear, e.g. they may reinforce avoidance and so inadvertently help in maintaining the response and therefore the fear.

Behavioural formulation

A fear or phobia may arise from a conditioned response to a traumatic event in an adolescent's life and may be maintained through avoidance and through reinforcement by others who help the adolescent to avoid the feared object or situation.

Behavioural intervention:

- **Systematic desensitisation**: this procedure involves muscle relaxation training, the use of an anxiety hierarchy and gradual exposure to the specific object or situation. An anxiety hierarchy ranges from the least-provoking situation to the most anxiety-provoking situation. Adolescents are encouraged to contemplate these anxiety-producing situations in a state of relaxation. This hierarchy can be produced through imagination or through real-life exposure. The aim is for the adolescent to overcome anxiety through gradually experiencing the stimulus as less and less threatening as he or she comes to perceive it as having no harmful effects.

- **Flooding**: this procedure involves presenting the fear-producing stimulus immediately, at full power. Again this can be done through imagination or real-life exposure. The usual response is then prevented. This method is questionable for use with children who may experience it as frightening.

- **Reinforcement**: a positive reinforcer is given to the adolescent when he or she approximate, to the desired behaviour, e.g. being near the feared object or situation. The desired behaviour is shaped through reinforcing successive approximations to the desired behaviour. The target behaviour needs to be clearly defined; the reinforcers must be made contingent, appropriate and provided immediately upon completion of the behaviour and be consistently applied.

- **Extinction**: this procedure occurs where reinforcement of a behaviour is discontinued. Parents and others should be asked to stop performing actions that encourage the adolescent to avoid the feared object or situation.

Problem: Depression

An adolescent is seen as depressed when there is a persistent and pervasive depressed mood which is characterised by feelings of worthlessness, helplessness and hopelessness. There may be associated physical symptoms, e.g. weight loss or gain, fatigue, insomnia and associated cognitive processes (suicidal thoughts) and associated behaviours (substance abuse).

Behavioural assessment

It is necessary to identify the antecedents of depressed moods, e.g. a bereavement in the family, family conflict, the loss of relationships with significant others, sexual abuse or depression in a parent. It is also necessary to identify the consequences of the depression, e.g. loss of peer friendships, difficulties at school, school absenteeism and substance abuse.

Behavioural formulation

Depression is seen as arising from the absence or insufficiency of reinforcement provided by significant others, e.g. parents, siblings and close friends. It may also arise from lack of social skills, in particular, those necessary for obtaining positive reinforcement from others. Once behaviours are no longer reinforced, behaviours are no longer performed.

Behavioural intervention

Social skills training involves modelling, role play with feedback, positive reinforcement, behaviour rehearsal and homework tasks.

Cognitive-behavioural approach

This approach emphasises the role cognitions and cognitive appraisal play in adolescent emotional difficulties. Emotional difficulties are often responses to an individual's cognitive processing of stimuli. Observation and measurement are still seen as necessary.

Ellis (1990) highlights the role of irrational beliefs in contributing to emotional difficulties. His **ABC analysis** helps to elucidate his approach. A is the activating event, B is the irrational belief that ensues and C are the emotional and behavioural consequences.

For example, an adolescent girl experiences rejection from her boyfriend (A) and from this jumps to the irrational belief that she is unattractive to all boys and will never be able to have romantic relationships again (B) and, as a result (C), becomes depressed and avoids boys.

Beck (1976) emphasises the role of distorted thinking in contributing to emotional difficulties. He describes a number of cognitive distortions that lead to difficulties, e.g.:

- **magnification**: making mountains out of molehills;
- **over-generalisation**: drawing a major conclusion from insufficient evidence;
- **selective abstraction**: paying attention to only some types of evidence.

Bandura (1977) emphasises the role of two kinds of expectations:

- **outcome expectations**: expectation that certain behaviours will bring about certain results;
- **efficacy expectations**: expectation that one is able to perform the behaviour successfully.

Low perceived self-efficacy contributes to feelings of being unable to cope and therefore emotional difficulties.

Schemas

A schema is an individual's structured way of organising and selecting information about events in the external world. Self-schemas are those that refer to an individual's self-concepts which may be positive or negative; positive if they interpret events optimistically or negative if pessimistically.

Cognitive appraisal and attribution

Cognitive appraisal occurs between stimuli and responses. A person thinks about the stimulus before deciding on which way to behave. This process involves particular memories, beliefs and expectations.

Attribution involves beliefs about the causes of particular events. There are three dimensions: **global/specific, stable/unstable, internal/external**:

- Adolescents may attribute problems to internal explanations (e.g. blaming themselves) or external explanations (e.g. blaming others).
- They may attribute problems to global explanations (e.g. they are useless in all situations) or specific explanations (e.g. they are useless only in this particular situation).
- They may attribute problems to stable explanations (e.g. never being able to achieve one's goals no matter what the time) or unstable explanations (e.g. unable to achieve the goal at that particular time).

Self-reinforcement

Mental reinforcers as well as external reinforcers can be used to shape particular behaviours, e.g. self-praise or self-criticism. These two forms of reinforcement can be linked in that self-praise or self-criticism can lead to rewarding oneself or punishing oneself.

Problem: Anxiety and phobias

Cognitive assessment

The aim is to identify the activating event (A) that activates a belief (B) that in turn contributes to the consequence (C), anxiety or phobia. This form of analysis depends on self-report and the idea of a 'fear thermometer' that enables an individual to rate his or her fear on a scale. Self-monitoring is another aspect of assessment which requires the individual to keep a record of his or her cognitions regarding the difficulty.

Cognitive interventions

- **Modelling (Bandura, 1977)**: this intervention requires a real or symbolic model to display coping skills along with calm in the situation where the phobic adolescent feels he or she would experience an anxiety reaction. The model ideally should be of the same sex, age and ethnicity as the adolescent, and should also display the qualities of competence and warmth.

- **Rational-emotive (Ellis, 1990)**: the antecedent or activating event that causes anxiety or phobia is identified. Following this identification the adolescent's irrational beliefs voiced in negative self-statements are in turn identified. The adolescent is encouraged to challenge these irrational beliefs and substitute positive and realistic self-statements.

- **Self-instructional training (Meichenbaum, 1977)**: an adolescent is encouraged to model him- or herself on an individual who successfully copes with anxiety or phobic provoking situations and who simultaneously voices positive self-statements.

Learning problems

The concept

Adolescents may experience learning and communication problems for a variety of reasons. They may suffer learning difficulties such as reading, numeracy and writing difficulties. In a severe form, reading difficulties may manifest themselves in the form of a specific reading disorder. Reading difficulties are frequently associated with behavioural problems. Some adolescents face academic problems such as lack of motivation for learning because of emotional and behavioural problems, especially problems with relationships which dominate their thinking. Sometimes adolescents cannot concentrate on their studies due to other problems such as drug experimentation. Learning is also affected when adolescents manifest behavioural difficulties which can arise because of peer pressure, concerns about financial difficulties or poor housing.

Types

Reading disorder is often defined as a reading achievement that is below the expected level for the child's age, education and intelligence and this impairment significantly interferes with academic success or daily activities that involve reading.

Before a child is diagnosed as having specific reading problems, other reasons for reading difficulties ought to be investigated such as inadequate schooling and hearing and visual impairments.

Mathematics disorder is a learning disorder. Four groups of impaired skills have been identified:

- **linguistic skills**: those related to understanding mathematical terms and converting written problems into mathematical symbols;
- **perceptual skills**: the ability to recognise and understand symbols and to order clusters of numbers;
- **mathematical skills**: basic addition, subtraction, multiplication and division, and following sequencing of basic operations;
- **attentional skills**: copying figures correctly and observing operational symbols correctly.

Other reasons for lack of arithmetic ability might be bad mathematical instruction, or lack of co-ordination in the adolescent.

Disorder of written expression is an impairment that affects a person whose writing skills are significantly below the expected level of age and education and intellectual capacity and can be diagnosed by a standardised test. The disorder interferes with the demands for writing in everyday life and affects educational performance.

Symptoms

If the above disorders are not diagnosed early so that the adolescent can receive specialist help, other symptoms might develop such as truancy, general disinterest in school work, attention deficit disorder and conduct disorder. Most children with learning disorders who are not diagnosed as having specific learning difficulties and then given appropriate help with reading, arithmetic or writing often have a sense of shame and humiliation because of their continuing failure and ongoing frustration. They might have a history of impaired speech, language and spelling problems and they might exhibit emotional and behavioural difficulties in the form of ADHD.

Such adolescents tend to be angry and depressed and exhibit poor self-esteem. They might even develop a chronic depressive disorder because of their growing sense of isolation, incompetence, estrangement and despair.

Treatment

Various methods are used:

- Referral to a specialist teacher who is qualified in special educational needs (SEN) and can develop a positive, supportive relationship with the adolescent.
- A special needs teacher (SENCO) can address the reading disorder through structured programmes, e.g. phonological awareness training. Parents can be involved through paired reading. Good study skills should be encouraged including time management (prioritising and scheduling activities), active reading and creating a cognitive map of newly acquired knowledge.

- Mathematical disorder can be treated by using materials that are appropriate to the particular adolescent. Computer programs can be helpful, as well as physical therapy and sensory integration activities.
- Disorder of written expression can be treated with intensive and continual administration of individually programmed one-to-one expressive and creative writing therapy.
- Referral to a counsellor or therapist who can address any co-existing emotional and behavioural difficulties through various therapeutic approaches, e.g. behavioural, cognitive-behavioural and person-centred counselling.
- Parental counselling can also help.

Academic problems

Many young people in schools, colleges and universities face a variety of academic problems which do not fall into the category of learning disorders, learning difficulties or learning problems. Academic problems in this context refer to problems of motivation, study and examinations. These academic problems vary from very minor difficulties to major problems and, as a result, studying and achievement are affected. Most young people in education want to achieve relatively good results and are usually proud of their achievements. Sometimes, however, problems arise that handicap progress and some students are not able to fulfil their potential.

Under-achievement is a major factor, and educationalists try at different intervals to find different and stimulating programmes to improve study skills, motivation and examination results. Sometimes students find the changes in the curriculum or the examination system confusing and alienating, but others try to accommodate to the changes and learn from their experiences.

Contributory factors to academic problems

Adolescents can experience difficulties in academic studies if their **general coping mechanisms** for a variety of developmental tasks are limited. The effectiveness of coping strategies is reduced where adolescents face emotional difficulties such as anxiety, depression, panic attacks, grief and stress.

Emotional difficulties can arise through the following: becoming independent, separation from parents even if they are looking forward to leaving home, adjusting to a new environment when changing schools, attending a new college or university, adapting to new and more demanding social situations, competing with peers, asserting themselves, making new relationships, especially intimate relationships, and learning new and unfamiliar ways of thinking about issues and ideas.

Anxiety may hamper adolescents' abilities to perform well in examinations and tests, to speak in small or large groups, to write essays or assignments, and to ask questions when they do not understand something. Adolescents who suffer from **depression** can withdraw from academic pursuits. Adolescents who face **family problems** such as parental marital conflicts, mental illness in a family member, financial difficulties, poor housing, overcrowded conditions, or relationship difficulties may be distracted and unable to study effectively.

Bereavement such as the death of a parent, the loss of a significant relationship or a change of teacher may result in **identity conflicts** for some adolescents. Some students do not have strong egos (stable sense of self) and find it difficult to prioritise their work, identify goals and finish their assignments; the lack of achievement can result in feelings of boredom and a sense that studies or even life are futile.

The **suffering and stress** in the lives of some adolescents might not be obvious to an observer. Some adolescents suffer mental, physical or even sexual abuse or exploitation. Some experience a sudden trauma like rape but cannot seek help out of their predicament for a variety of reasons such as feelings of shame, or fear of not being believed. Some are competitive and envious, others are not able to study alone, and others cannot study in conditions that distract their concentration.

Some adolescents suffer from **physical illnesses** that are not easily diagnosed such as thyroid problems, anaemia, eating disorders or sleeplessness, and, as a result, they are not able to study effectively. Some who resort to substance abuse like illicit drug-taking and others who become dependent on alcohol find it difficult to concentrate on their studies.

Some adolescents face difficulties for **academic reasons**. When academic problems arise, adolescents often state the following reasons for their **motivational difficulties**:

- The course is too difficult or too easy.
- They have a personal dislike of a teacher or supervisor.
- Lessons/lectures are not stimulating enough so their interest is not captured.
- They are following the wrong course for their interest or aptitude.
- They are distracted by something else in their lives that seems more imminent or urgent.
- There is a psychological difficulty that hinders progress, either in themselves or significant others.
- They are frightened of competition or competing beyond their capabilities.

Some of the other reasons for academic problems are related to **study difficulties**:

- They are not clear how to write or structure essays, assignments, dissertations, or theses.
- They leave their studying to the last minute so they do not have enough time.
- They are not able to organise their material.

- They are not able to plan their work.
- They are overwhelmed by the amount they have to do.

Some of the reasons why students find **examinations** difficult are:

- They have not revised.
- The revision they have followed is inappropriate.
- They are so frightened of examinations that they feel paralysed and thus unable to think clearly and coherently.
- They have a fear of failure or fear of success.

Methods that can help adolescents study more effectively include:

- early diagnosis of problem;
- an appropriate choice of course and subjects;
- appropriate academic support, e.g. guidance on how to take notes, write essays, do experiments, structure the work;
- referral to the appropriate department for specific help, e.g. learning difficulties;
- appropriate boundaries, e.g. meeting deadlines, attending lessons regularly and on time, behaving appropriately in lessons;
- clear and firm disciplinary procedures;
- effective pastoral support, e.g. monitoring of academic progress and welfare;
- referral to a counsellor for emotional or behavioural problems;
- help with financial or accommodation difficulties;
- referral to appropriate agencies for specific problems, e.g. social services for abused adolescents or poor housing;
- referral to GP for illnesses;
- parental interest and involvement;
- parents and teachers providing support and encouragement.

Adolescent relationship problems

The concept

Most adolescents experience problems with relationships, such as with parents, siblings, relatives, friends, peers, girlfriends, boyfriends and people in authority.

Particular manifestations of adolescent problems with relationships:

- arguments with parents culminating in feelings of anger, hostility, depression and rejection;
- jealousy and rivalry, e.g. of siblings and peers;
- idealisation, e.g. regarding some person such as an uncle as perfect and wonderful and comparing their parents unfavourably to this person;

- hostility, e.g. regarding another person as unpleasant and nasty and ignoring the existence of those attributes that do not fit into the picture;
- social isolation and loneliness;
- competitiveness or withdrawal, shyness or preoccupation with peers;
- in love or out of love, obsessed with a boyfriend or girlfriend;
- opposition and hostility to authority figures.

Many negative relationships result from:

- lack of or inadequate communication;
- conflicts of material interests;
- disappointments and incompatibility;
- very high expectations or very low ones, particularly low self-esteem;
- differing priorities;
- moral conflicts;
- lack of respect for others;
- the generation gap.

Many adolescents test boundaries by doing the following:

- abusing substances such as drugs and alcohol, e.g. cannabis, ecstasy, heroin, amphetamines and cocaine;
- engaging in deviant and delinquent behaviour, e.g. drunkenness, truanting, shoplifting, illegal driving;
- experimenting with sex, particularly risky or unsafe sex;
- disobeying parental rules that result in conflict, e.g. staying out late at night, using the telephone excessively, refusing to tidy up, wearing certain clothes or fashions;
- being inconsiderate, e.g. playing loud music.

Separation

Many adolescents find the loss of a relationship difficult to cope with, whether separation is through death or rejection. Some degree of separation anxiety is inevitable and it is an expected part of a child's normal development, e.g. an infant separating from mother, or a child starting school for the first time. Separation anxiety disorder is the most common anxiety in childhood and it manifests itself in excessive worry regarding separation from the major attachment figure.

Some children and adolescents experience separation from their parents as difficult. They imagine that they will be left alone, unprotected, and that they will not be able to cope without the support of their significant others. They may experience being away from a significant other (e.g. mother), even for a few hours, as a rejection by the mother.

Symptoms of separation anxiety:

- refusal to go to school;
- fear and distress at separation;
- repeated complaints of physical symptoms such as headaches and stomach-aches when separation is anticipated;
- nightmares related to separation issues.

This form of anxiety only occurs in 1 per cent of adolescents, e.g. some adolescents exhibit some of these symptoms when anticipating leaving home.

Loss of a relationship

Some adolescents experience the premature ending of an important relationship as devastating. They can become very depressed if a friend moves away or they themselves move home or a boyfriend or girlfriend ends the relationship. They can feel depressed if friends switch allegiance or friends decide they need more space and do not phone or see the adolescent as often as they did before.

Some adolescents experience feelings of rejection when their parents divorce or separate and believe that they have lost the parent who has moved out of the parental home. Some experience grief at the loss of a relationship and the symptoms are similar to those experienced at a bereavement.

Bereavement

Symptoms of bereavement:

- inconsolable crying or shock, resulting in numbness;
- deep sadness, resulting in withdrawn behaviour where nothing seems to matter;
- denial of any sad feelings, where the adolescent might behave as if nothing has happened;
- under-achievement occurring after academic success;
- anger projected (directed) at others, e.g. towards a parent, teacher or a friend and sometimes towards strangers;
- feelings of inadequacy, guilt, self-blame, despair.

Bereavement is a complex issue for adolescents. They want to feel in control of their emotions and often deny the significance of events in their lives. Many adolescents who exhibit some of the above symptoms might have had a parent die years before and they do not associate their symptoms with grieving.

Adolescents experience the loss of a significant relationship as rejection. Rejection is one of the major causes of depression and many adolescents can become isolated, uncommunicative and withdrawn as a result of bereavement.

Treatment

Individual or group counselling where the adolescent is given time and space to grieve. The counsellor ought to:

- actively listen to the adolescent's feelings and encourage the adolescent to express pain, despair, anger, guilt and the many other feelings that might be difficult to articulate;
- allow the adolescent to make meaning of his or her experience by helping him or her to recognise that denial, depression, anger and projection of the unexpressed feelings are part of the process of grief;
- encourage relaxation exercises which may help the adolescent feel more in control of his or her anxiety.

Defences

Adolescents employ many defence mechanisms when they face difficulties, especially difficulties with relationships. The following defences can be identified:

denial	adolescents deny the existence of problems or difficulties and persuade themselves that something is not so in the hope that it will go away, e.g. they might be not getting on well with their siblings but they might pretend that this is not so.
distortion	they can accept that they have problems or difficulties but they might make light of them, e.g. they are upset by the ending of a relationship but they convince themselves that they are not upset, insisting that they are upset about something entirely different.
displacement	diverting emotional feelings from one person or object to another, e.g. the adolescent feels angry about his or her mother's death and displaces that anger on to a teacher.
projection	attributing personal shortcomings and failures to other people or the environment, e.g. angry with a teacher for allegedly discriminating against them but they are really upset with themselves for under-achieving by not studying hard enough.
rationalising	a means of self-deception where adolescents find satisfactory and socially acceptable reasons for their conduct, e.g. they feel they must take drugs or drink when in company with peers otherwise they will be rejected.
regression	reversion to the past or to an earlier childhood state, where the yearning seems to be a return to the state of dependency where the adolescent feels protected and has decisions made for him or her, e.g. the adolescent refuses to grow up, mature and take on responsibilities. Sometimes this regressive tendency might be actively encouraged by parents who do not want their children to grow up and leave home.

withdrawal   the adolescent retires emotionally from any given situation by day-dreaming or becoming apathetic, e.g. rather than recognise the pain of separation because of parents' divorce.

The ways in which adults can help adolescents cope with difficult relationships include:

- The relationship that is causing most stress for the adolescent or the parent ought to be identified and talked about; sometimes a change in attitude can resolve the problem.

- Sometimes the only solution is to accept the differences between people and try to keep a positive attitude but sometimes drastic action needs to take place, e.g. the adolescent needs to change school or leave home.

- Before any dramatic changes take place the parties involved could try to compromise by talking through their grievances and finding ways to alleviate the stress by the use of an unwritten contract, e.g. the parent would allow the adolescent to go to a party on the Saturday night and the adolescent only uses the telephone for an hour per evening.

- Sometimes it might be useful if the person in authority, e.g. the teacher or parent can name the adolescent's unmanageable feelings rather than tell them off for unacceptable behaviour, e.g. the adolescent might be caught taking drugs but the real problem might be because the adolescent finds it difficult to grieve because of the ending of a relationship or because of jealousy of a sibling.

Adolescents respond to a consistent, firm and caring approach where the boundaries are clear and articulated.

It is important for the adolescent to feel that he or she is loved, cared for, supported and contained.

Self-esteem problems

The concept

Self-esteem is a complex issue and can be seen as a function or a component of the personality, and a person's identity and awareness. Most people have positive or negative cognitive, emotional and behaviour reactions towards themselves and others. There is the self that one sees or perceives as the **real self**, even if it is hidden, and there is also the self that one wishes to be, the **ideal self**. It is a subjective experience where judgement of worthiness is expressed in the personal attitudes of the individual. Self-esteem is dynamic in that it can change over time. Lack of competence can also affect self-esteem. Self-esteem can be seen as a developmental process or product and it can also be seen as global or situational and it has defensive or protective functions.

Parental factors that affect the development of self-esteem include parental love and involvement and parental acceptance. Well-defined and realistic, but high parental expectations and clear limits as well as authoritative and consistent approach are important. The personal factors that affect self-esteem include having a positive outlook, being self-directed and autonomous. However, high self-esteem may have negative qualities in that there may be difficulty in seeing and acknowledging one's weaknesses.

Types

There are different types of low self-esteem, such as feelings of inferiority, unworthiness, loneliness and insecurity. Another type of low self-esteem is one where there is defensiveness or over-sensitivity. Those people who have low self-esteem find it difficult to tolerate and cope with stress. Furthermore, they are likely to suffer from anxiety and depression and engage in substance abuse and anti-social behaviour.

Identity

Self-esteem is seen as closely linked to a person's **identity**. The self is seen as the totality of the person. Esteem is seen as the value one attributes to one's self or another. Thus, self-esteem is how one evaluates or judges one's self and identity is the sense of one's self as a unique individual. Adolescents between the ages of 12 and 18 establish an idea of who they are, and find their roles and their values. When adolescents are confused about their value and role, they go through an identity crisis.

Approaches

Psychodynamic approach
Adolescents with high self-esteem have a strong ego and are better able to deal with anxiety and the demands of reality. Adolescents with a weak ego lack the ability to deal with impulse and with reality and instead make use of defensive measures, thus failing to grow emotionally and develop.

Behavioural approach
Children and adolescents learn they are valuable human beings because their parents regard them with affection; they develop high standards because these are consistently reinforced by parents. Children also model themselves on the positive or negative behaviours of their parents and peers.

Cognitive approach
This approach sees negative self-esteem as a consequence of irrational beliefs or cognitive distortions whereby self-evaluation is influenced or associated with illogical, non-empirical and non-pragmatic beliefs.

Interventions

Factors relating to increasing self-esteem include acceptance, and caring and positive feedback.

Raising self-esteem can be achieved through:

- cognitive restructuring
- reattribution training
- assertiveness training
- modelling

improving problem-solving skills.

Adolescent sexual relationships

The concept

Human sexual behaviour is socially and culturally diverse and determined by many different factors. It is affected by one's relationships, life circumstances and culture. Sexuality is part of one's personality, biological make-up and sense of identity. The adolescent's quest to establish an identity intensifies the conflicts that arise due to the young person's explorations of personality and sexuality (psychosexuality). Sexual orientation, i.e. hetero-, homo- and bisexuality, is not necessarily fixed but can undergo change depending on age and context.

Types of adolescent sexual problems and anxieties

Exploration of sexual identity can lead adolescents to do the following:

- question their gender identity, their sexual orientation and their sexual behaviour;
- have doubts about their sexual attractiveness;
- experience conflicts between love and sex;
- experience conflicts between their sexual desires and their religious beliefs;
- engage in multiple sexual relationships;
- become pregnant and be faced with the question of abortion;
- contract a sexually transmitted disease (STD) and fear HIV/AIDS.

Characteristics of adolescents with sexual anxieties:

- dressing in an understated way, hiding their bodies in very loose clothes, i.e. in order to avoid feeling sexual and being thought of as sexual;
- dressing in an explicitly sexual way, i.e. in order to confirm one's sexual attractiveness especially where one doubts one's attractiveness;
- having many sexual contacts, i.e. in order to reassure oneself that one is attractive;
- fear of sex (due to religious or moral considerations);

- guilt feelings after sex, e.g. for religious reasons or breaking parents' moral code;

- ending up in vulnerable or risky situations, e.g. getting drunk or high on drugs in order to alleviate feelings of anxiety when faced with sexual situations;

- behavioural disturbances such as vandalism, violence, truancy and theft in order to cope with doubts about one's masculinity or femininity;

- eating disorders might be related to anxieties over sexuality;

- withdrawn or aggressive behaviour can mask feelings of fear, humiliation, confusion, shame and rage that result from being sexually abused or assaulted.

Sexual orientation

With the approach of puberty young people experience the upsurge of sex hormones and sexual curiosity is intensified. Adolescents are physically capable of coitus and orgasm but many are inhibited by parental attitudes, social restraints or religious beliefs. They face a dual problem of establishing their sexual identities and controlling their sexual impulses. It is very likely that at this juncture of their lives they will begin to reflect on their sexual orientation. Sexual response is a psychophysiological experience where arousal is triggered by both psychological and physical stimuli.

Sexual orientation: This describes the object of the person's sexual impulses, i.e. a heterosexual is sexually attracted to a person of the opposite sex; a homosexual is sexually attracted to a person of the same sex and a bisexual is sexually attracted to people of both sexes. A particular sexual orientation may be a temporary or an enduring state of affairs, e.g. adolescents may engage in a homosexual phase during their teens and become heterosexual afterwards or they may continue their homosexuality.

Homosexuality: Recent studies indicate that genetic and biological components may contribute to homosexual orientation. Some adolescents experiment with relationships and have sex with people of the same sex and by the end of adolescence they begin to form intimate relationships with people from the opposite sex. Some adolescents find it difficult to think that they might be homosexual; they deny their feelings and insist wholeheartedly that they are heterosexual. Social attitudes towards homosexuality would force them into this position. It was only in 1973 that homosexuality was eliminated as a diagnostic category by the American Psychiatric Association and was removed from DSM-IV. With this kind of background some adolescents see homosexuality as a pathological disorder and when homosexual feelings arise, deny or reject them. Some over-compensate by engaging in an exaggerated masculinity or femininity.

Bisexuality: Some adolescents are sexually attracted to both sexes. It is difficult for some adolescents to come to terms with the thought that they are sexually attracted to both males and females. Some see it as having the best of both worlds, but some cannot cope with feelings that seem to show ambivalence or at least not a preference for one rather than another.

Heterosexuality: Most adolescents say they are heterosexual and fear being labelled by their peers as homosexual. They see being heterosexual as being normal, i.e. boys wish to be seen as being attracted to girls and girls wish to be seen as being attracted to boys. Heterosexuality is defined as the norm socially, culturally and religiously and is not generally perceived as a problem.

Treatment for sexual difficulties

One way to treat sexual difficulties is through various forms of psychotherapy, e.g. cognitive-behavioural as well as psychodynamic. Adolescents are often more anxious about sexual attractiveness, sexual normality and sexual orientation than sexual dysfunctions, but when a sexual dysfunction is identified such as erectile disorders, then a referral to the GP or a psychiatrist is necessary. Ethical, religious and cultural issues and controversies arise with regard to sexuality and these need to be discussed and clarified when considering the question of treatment.

Types of therapy

classic psychodynamic theory	tells us that sexual difficulties arise from early developmental conflicts. Thus, any sexual difficulty can be treated as an emotional problem that occurs as a result of unresolved Oedipal relationships with one's parents.
psychodynamic therapy	will focus on the exploration of unconscious conflicts. Through insight those conflicts can be resolved allowing the individual to cope with his or her sexual impulses in a more acceptable way and also enabling the individual to find appropriate channels for those impulses.
behavioural therapy	a way to work with some sexual problems, e.g. fear of sex is treated through using behavioural techniques where the particular sexual problem is addressed. The therapist can see the client as being anxious about sexual performance and can reflect on the situation as he or she sees it rather than interpret underlying dynamics. Sexual dysfunction often seems to involve lack of information, misinformation and performance anxieties. Behavioural techniques such as systematic desensitisation can be used; this is where the therapist sets up a hierarchy of anxiety-provoking situations for the client from the least threatening to the most anxiety-making. Specific

exercises can be prescribed which address the problem of the individual from the very mildest anxiety such as the thought of the client talking to a person of the opposite sex to the most anxious-making such as penetrative sex. The therapist would enable the client to master each anxiety. The programme would encourage behaviours that do not arouse anxiety by inhibiting the learned anxious response.

Other methods that might help an adolescent recognise and cope with anxieties can be:

relaxation exercises   where adolescents learn to relax their muscles at the initial onset of anxiety;

assertiveness training   where adolescents learn to express sexual needs openly and without fear and refuse sexual requests that seem unreasonable;

group therapy   where adolescents in a group with their peers can explore their feelings of shame, anxiety, guilt and gather accurate information as well as enhance self-esteem and self-acceptance.

Teenage pregnancy and parenthood

Some teenage pregnancies are unwanted and can cause upheaval in the family. Adolescents usually find themselves in difficult situations and prompt decisions have to be made as to whether the teenage girl will go ahead with having the baby, give the baby up for adoption or terminate the pregnancy. Sometimes the father of the baby is involved and wants to be supportive and take responsibility, but sometimes the teenage girl is left to make her own decisions and rely either on her family or friends for support, or on the social services. There have been some tragic cases of girls giving birth in circumstances that are dangerous to both the baby and themselves.

According to the English Conception Statistics, the under-18-year-old conception rate for 2001 was 3.5 per cent lower than in 2000, and was 10 per cent below the 1998 rate, which is an encouraging movement towards the target of a 15 per cent reduction by 2004. The under-16-year-old conception rate for 2001 was 4.5 per cent lower than the 2000 rate, and was 11 per cent below the 1998 rate. The percentage of conceptions leading to abortion rose to 46.0 per cent for under-18s, and 55.9 per cent for under-16s, continuing the upward trend observed since 1995.

What are some of the reasons for teenage pregnancy?
- ignorance of contraception;
- lack of sex education;

- carelessness, in that contraception is not taken seriously;
- contraception is not effective;
- need to prove fertility;
- need to have someone to love;
- way of keeping the partner in a relationship;
- way of punishing the parents for real or imagined wrongs;
- as a gift to parents or partner;
- attention-seeking behaviour;
- envy of the parents' ability to be creative;
- because of either real or internalised negative experiences when they were babies, they want a baby to love and care for in a way they would have liked to have been looked after as babies;
- as a form of teenage rebellion;
- assertion of their adulthood and independence;
- having a sex life which is regarded an adult mode of behaviour;
- promiscuity for psychological reasons.

Why do some teenagers choose termination?

There are teenagers who are not ready for parenthood for a variety of reasons. Some of these reasons can be:

- fear of displeasing parents or partner if they keep the baby;
- unwillingness to prejudice education or a future career;
- unwillingness to give up social life and friends;
- partner is not committed to the relationship or the possible baby;
- illness;
- fear of pregnancy or the fear of the actual birth experience.

Sometimes teenagers choose termination because they feel pressure from parents or friends or partner to terminate the pregnancy. They are often persuaded that this is the best option for them and they go ahead with an abortion before they come to terms with what this might mean to them. There are teenagers who abort who develop psychological problems as a result and suffer from nightmares, guilt feelings, anger and anxiety. Some who take some time to consider the decision by allowing themselves to talk through their feelings, fantasies and fears are more likely to resolve some of their confusing and difficult feelings and be more informed.

Helping teenagers avoid pregnancy

Teenagers need to learn about intimate relationships, sex and contraception. There are those who can be reluctant to learn or take advice from adults. They feel adults are old-fashioned and authoritarian and some teenagers want to experiment and find out about relationships and sex themselves. Some feel grown up; others, however, feel immature, and avoid discussing these issues with their parents or their teachers. Sometimes parents are too embarrassed or too awkward to discuss sex or contraception with their children and sometimes parents imagine that their children are too young to discuss these subjects.

- Sex education at school is hugely important. Teenagers will listen to someone charismatic who is emotionally separate and able to articulate in a clear and informative way about the subject.
- Parental discussion can be important if parents are able to discuss the matter of sex education in a detached way and give their children a good informative book to read at their leisure which can encourage discussion.
- Teenagers are helped by discussing their changing hormones with an approachable GP or school or college counsellor who can have informative literature on display in the office and the reception area and who will take time to listen kindly and discuss the teenager's questions and queries.
- Teenage magazines are useful in that they often advertise organisations that are able to give information and advice and discuss contraception, sexual maturity, relationships, STDs, HIV and AIDS and help young people understand their physical and psychological welfare.

Parenthood

Teenage parenthood can be problematic when young people are not mature enough to be totally committed to looking after a baby. These teenagers need time to grow up themselves and develop physical and emotional maturity before they are ready to take on responsibility.

Some teenagers are, however, very capable of taking on the parental role but, in some cases, their own development will suffer.

What do teenagers need to help them cope with a baby?

Loving the baby is often not enough. Teenagers also need to have:

- supportive parents, partners, friends and professionals;
- enough money, either through social funds or parental financial support;
- self-awareness, relative confidence, knowledge of baby development;
- a strong ego and commitment to bringing up the baby;
- the provision of information and support from the appropriate bodies.

Mental health problems

Substance abuse

Substance abuse is where actual drug use leads to physical or mental health deterioration. Drug dependence, on the other hand, is compulsive use that may result in physical changes that are the effects of tolerance and withdrawal. In the case of adolescents, persistent substance abuse can lead to criminal activity, cognitive impairment, educational failure and difficulties in maintaining long-term relationships. The children of substance abusers may themselves suffer from drug-related problems, e.g. HIV infection and foetal alcohol syndrome.

Experimental and recreational use of drugs is fairly prevalent among adolescents particularly with respect to cigarettes, alcohol, ecstasy and cannabis. However, there is a growing problem with drugs such as solvents, heroin and cocaine. There are those who are chronic abusers, those who are occasional users and those who use drugs daily and at weekends. Polydrug use, i.e. drugs taken separately or together in a cocktail, is not unusual. Chronic early polydrug use is connected to more difficulties than experimental use but only a small minority of adolescent drug users go on to become abusers.

Harmful effects of drug abuse depend on the drug taken. With respect to stimulants and hallucinogens, high heartbeat rate (tachycardia), high blood pressure (hypertension), irregular heart rhythms (arrhythmias) and seizures can occur.

Hallucinogen use can also lead to flashbacks and psychotic states. In the case of alcohol, solvents and opioids, stupor and coma can occur. Withdrawal from drugs can lead to physiological problems (coma and seizures) and drug abuse can also lead to medical complications (liver, kidney damage) and through the use of non-sterile injections to hepatitis and AIDS. Accidental over-use or drug impurities can lead to fatalities. At home, drug use can lead to conflict with parents, and at school or college, conflict with the authorities and educational failure. Drug users may also become involved with the youth justice system.

Drug abuse can co-occur with other disorders such as conduct disorder and mood disorders.

The main theories of drug abuse are:

- **biological** (temperament for risk-taking and rule-breaking behaviour) including pharmacological aspects (tolerance, dependence and withdrawal effects of drugs);
- **psychodynamic** (self-medication, insecure attachment, low self-esteem, unfulfilled dependency needs and search for an adult identity);
- **behavioural** (positive and negative reinforcement effects of drug use);
- **family systems** (modelling of parents' drug use and attitudes towards use, disorganised family life and lack of parenting skills);
- **multi-systemic risk** (temperament, early behavioural problems, early onset of use, educational failure, family drug-taking, family conflict, poor parenting, early peer rejection, deviant peer group, drug availability, positive attitudes towards use and neighbourhood disorganisation);
- **sociological** (deprived neighbourhood, deviant drug-taking peer subculture, alienation and deprivation from the wider community and easy availability of drugs).

Interventions

Family therapy consists of helping parents form a strong alliance, to maintain boundaries between themselves and their children, to practise effective supervision, to develop problem-solving strategies and conflict-resolution skills.

Multi-systemic family therapy aims to change drug use by focusing on the family but also on the individual, the peer group, the school and the community.

Self-harm

See also Chapter 5.

Self-harm is where people intentionally and habitually inflict damage to their bodies. It is behaviour that usually has its onset during adolescence and mainly affects young females and those women in their twenties or thirties. Certain groups self-harm more than others, e.g. gay men and women and those with learning disabilities. Types of self-harm include cutting, making incisions and scratching the skin and hitting and inflicting burns on the body.

Many who self-harm are attempting to cope with unbearable emotions and hope to achieve emotional self-healing or to feel relief. It can also be an attempt to gain a sense of self-control. For some it can be a means of expressing grief, despair, anger, frustration and protest. Self-harm can also serve as self-punishment or punishment of others and as a way of communicating with others. The reaction of others can be shock and alarm, some blaming themselves. A common factor in self-harm is childhood sexual abuse.

Theories

Psychoanalytic theories see self-harm as a form of partial suicide, as a means of relieving guilt for illicit activities, as a result of loss or separation, as a representation of early psychological pain or as an internalised process of early object relations.

Schizophrenia

Schizophrenia is a persistent and diverse disorder of thought and perception. It can be characterised by delusions of thought insertion, withdrawal and broadcasting and also by culturally inappropriate delusions such as claiming to be a great religious or political figure or having superhuman abilities. There are also auditory hallucinations (hearing voices) along with incoherent thought or speech. The sufferer often becomes socially isolated as well as socially awkward, apathetic, emotionally flat, lacking in will and displays a paucity and poverty of speech. There is evidence that schizophrenics also suffer downward social drift, dropping down to a lower social level. There is cognitive impairment in the form of memory, attention, concept formation and executive functions.

Schizophrenia is rare in childhood but increases significantly during adolescence. The average age of onset is 18 to 25 for males and 26 to 45 for females. Early onset is associated with a poor prognosis for the future. Males develop the disorder on average five years before females and people who develop the condition are more likely to be born during the winter months.

It is the case that schizophrenic-like symptoms can be produced by certain drugs such as amphetamines which in large doses can cause delusions and hallucinations through over-stimulation of the dopamine system.

Biological factors including genetics are thought to play a significant part in the development of schizophrenia but not absolutely so as concordance is not 100 per cent but 50 per cent for monozygotic twins and 10 per cent for dizygotic twins. Some twins families have no history of schizophrenia whatsoever. There are no biological markers for schizophrenia and the mode of inheritance is unknown, which makes it difficult for genetic studies of the disorder. Currently the cause of schizophrenia is unknown.

Interventions

Schizophrenia sufferers may resist psychiatric examination and having a sufferer in the family can adversely affect family life, leading to conflict and stress among family members.

Biological or drug therapy through antipsychotics or neuroleptics is the usual treatment. Drugs are given by mouth or through depot injections. They can relieve delusions, hallucinations and disorganised thinking by blocking dopamine receptors. There can be adverse side-effects such as involuntary muscle contractions (dystonia), restlessness (akathisia) and tremors, stiffness and a mask-like face (pseudo-Parkinsonism) and uncontrollable face movements (tardive dyskinesia). These side-effects may persuade the sufferer to cease taking medication. However, many of these side-effects can be controlled. Newer drugs like Clozapine and Risperidone have fewer side-effects. Non-compliance is a significant factor in drug therapy varying from 20 to 50 per cent. This can be due to paranoid thinking, the adverse side-effects of drugs and a disorganised lifestyle.

Non-biological interventions that are seen as adjuncts to drug therapy include cognitive-behavioural therapy (cognitive restructuring and social skills training) and behavioural family therapy (education, communication and problem-solving skills). It has been shown that negative family attitudes and expressed emotion have an influence on the course of schizophrenia leading to an increased relapse rate. Family therapy can address these concerns and lead to a reduction in relapses. Relapse can also be due to other family problems, non-compliance with medication and co-occurrence with drug abuse.

Obsessive Compulsive Disorders (OCD)

These disorders are characterised by persistent, intrusive, recurrent obsessional thoughts and covert (cognitive) or overt (behavioural) compulsions that the sufferer finds distressing. These may take the form of washing/cleaning compulsions (mainly female), checking compulsions (males and females), list-making (males and females), hoarding and ruminations, persistent and unproductive thinking about personal matters or religious and philosophical themes. Obsessional thoughts include those about contamination, disasters, illness, death, order and forbidden sexual thoughts.

Obsessions and compulsions can occur separately. It is a relatively rare disorder. The onset is usually in adolescence before the age of 25 and occurs earlier in males than females. Many people have obsessions and compulsion but do not find them distressing and do not experience them as interfering with their social, familial and working lives. Children and adolescents who suffer from OCD are as likely to be compulsive cleaners and checkers as adults. The sufferer has insight and recognises that these thoughts and actions are voluntary but unnecessary. However, he or she finds it impossible to resist them permanently without becoming extremely anxious. These disorders often occur with anxiety, depression, sleeping problems, tics and occasionally aggressiveness. Symptoms similar to OCD can result from brain damage. Although there are people with obsessional personalities, most of these do not develop the disorder.

The family can be adversely affected through the sufferer dominating family life and demanding that other family members observe certain prohibitions or perform certain actions such as cleaning and washing rituals. Many family members at first resist then comply for the sake of peace and quiet. The result of OCD can be social isolation and restriction of social activities. It can also lead to separation and divorce.

Factors linked to the onset of the disorder include depression, shyness, illness, death or illness of a relative.

Approaches

Theoretical perspectives include the biological, psychoanalytical, behavioural and the cognitive-behavioural and family systems.

Biological approaches suggest basal ganglia problems and levels of the neurotransmitter serotonin as contributory factors.

Psychoanalytical approaches see OCD as a defensive reaction against repressed sexual and aggressive impulses that emerge during toilet training, these impulses creating anxiety which is then managed through undoing rituals.

Behavioural approaches regard OCD as learned or acquired, resulting from stimuli that elicit anxiety through classical conditioning. Certain compulsive rituals are found to reduce anxiety. The individual learns to repeat and maintain those rituals as a way of reducing anxiety thereby making the rituals into a habit.

Cognitive-behavioural approaches see irrational beliefs as the basis for obsessions and compulsions beliefs, e.g. an exaggerated sense of responsibility for potentially catastrophic events.

Family systems see family–child interactions as maintaining compulsive behaviour especially through those interactions serving to meet some of the needs of individual family members. Beliefs about the child's obsessions and compulsions may also contribute to them being maintained.

Interventions

Biological or drug therapy is used in severe cases and involves prescribing a drug such as clomipramine or a serotonin re-uptake inhibitor such as fluoxetine (Prozac). With drugs there can be side-effects such as mouth dryness, constipation, dizziness, drowsiness and nausea. The effectiveness of drugs depends on the continuation of medication as relapse can occur if drugs are terminated.

Behavioural interventions include *in vivo* or imaginal exposure (placing sufferers in a compulsive situation or asking them to imagine such a situation) and response prevention (refraining from performing the compulsive ritual) along with anxiety management training and parent training. The aim is for the sufferer to extinguish the anxiety that comes with not performing the compulsions. Exposure can also be used with obsessional thinking through habituation training. Modelling and reassurance by the therapist are also elements of this approach. Other behavioural techniques include systematic desensitisation (gradual exposure) and contingency management (avoiding positive reinforcement of compulsive behaviour) and muscle relaxation.

Cognitive-behavioural approaches are varied. Rational-emotive behaviour therapy (REBT) aims to challenge and change irrational beliefs relating to compulsions, e.g. an exaggerated sense of responsibility and those relating to obsessions, e.g. attaching significance to intrusive and repetitive thoughts. This is achieved by examining the logical, empirical and pragmatic bases for an individual's irrational beliefs. Other cognitive approaches include thought stopping (suddenly interrupting obsessional thinking with a loud command: 'Stop!') and distraction (engaging in alternative activities that distract).

Depression

Depression has a range of symptoms including persistent sadness and despair, diminished interest or pleasure in social, leisure and sexual activities, weight loss or gain, sleep disturbances, restlessness, fatigue, feelings of worthlessness and hopelessness, lack of concentration, indecision, recurring thoughts of death or suicide ideation and negative views of other people, the world and the future.

As well as these symptoms there is often a deterioration in family and peer relationships and in school or college achievement.

Depression is not rare but is more common among adolescents than children and often occurs along with other disorders such as those of anxiety and conduct. It is more common among adolescent girls than boys.

Approaches

Theories include biological, psychoanalytical, behavioural, cognitive-behavioural and family systems.

Biological approaches refer to a genetic predisposition and to a variety of biochemical factors that contribute to depressive disorders such as posited dysregulations of the amine, endocrine and immune systems.

Psychoanalytical approaches consider contributory factors to be self-directed aggression, low self-esteem due to perceived discrepancies between the actual self and an unrealistic ego ideal that is due to over-critical and perfectionist parenting, the loss of attachment relationships and the failure to master achievement tasks.

Behavioural approaches consider contributory factors to be loss of positive reinforcement and reinforcers due to the lack of appropriate social skills for eliciting reinforcement and reinforcers.

Cognitive-behavioural approaches consider factors such as negative cognitive-processing schemas and associated cognitive distortions, the lack of self-monitoring, self-evaluation and self-reinforcement skills and a depressive attributional style, i.e. making internal, global, stable attributions for failure but external, specific and unstable attributions for success.

Systems approaches consider systemic factors such as the family system and the school system. With regard to the family, negative family interactions may prevent the completion of appropriate developmental tasks. The disruption of family relationships may occur through parental loss, parental conflict, separation, parental psychiatric problems and parental criminality and parental alcohol and drug abuse. In addition, parent–adolescent conflict may contribute to depression.

With regard to school or college, contributory factors can be bullying, sexism and racism. The pastoral systems in educational institutions may be inadequate in not detecting bullying, sexism or racism and leaving them unchecked.

Interventions

Biological approaches focus on drug therapy. This involves prescribing tricyclic anti-depressants or selective serotonin re-uptake inhibitors (SSRIs). Tricyclic anti-depressants have doubtful efficacy for adolescents and also have serious side-effects. Other types of anti-depressant drugs can also have serious side-effects.

Behavioural approaches focus on equipping adolescents with appropriate social skills that enables them to elicit positive reinforcers and positive reinforcement.

Cognitive-behavioural approaches focus on psychoeducation, pleasant event scheduling, relaxation skills, challenging negative thinking and negative automatic thoughts, self-reinforcement, attribution retraining and problem-solving skills training.

Anxiety

Fear and anxiety are adaptive responses to threatening situations or perceived threats. Adaptive responses are based on an accurate assessment of potential risk or danger whereas a maladaptive response is based on an inaccurate assessment. Anxiety has physiological (physical arousal), affective (tense feelings), cognitive (perceived as threatening) and behavioural (avoidance) components.

Types of anxiety include simple phobias, separation anxiety, test anxiety and post-traumatic-stress disorder. Types of anxiety tending to appear first in adolescence include generalised anxiety, social anxiety, panic attacks and agoraphobia. Many experience more than one type of anxiety. More females than males experience separation anxiety, phobias, generalised anxiety and panic attacks. Anxiety co-occurs with other disorders such as conduct, ADHD and depression. In all cases of anxiety there is a heightened awareness or hyper-vigilance for situations that are seen as threatening or dangerous and a desire to avoid those situations. Avoidance behaviour may bring the adolescent into conflict with parents, peers and teachers. Factors contributing to anxiety include low self-esteem, an external locus of control, anxious attachment, exposure to carer anxiety, loss or separation from carers or peers, changing school, bullying and moving away from the neighbourhood.

Approaches

Biological approaches focus on the dysregulation of neurotransmitter systems, e.g. gamma-aminobutyric acid (GABA) for phobic and generalised anxiety and the adrenergic-noradrenergic for panic attacks. There is also believed to be a genetic predisposition for anxiety disorders.

Psychoanalytical approaches regard anxiety as arising due to the displacement of morally unacceptable impulses onto specific substitute objects or onto all available objects.

Cognitive approaches see anxiety as due to threatening events activating depressogenic cognitive schema or a mind-set that interprets the environment as threatening or involving cognitive distortions that construe situations as dangerous.

Behavioural approaches see phobias as being the result of classical conditioning.

Family systems approaches see anxiety within the family as arising through modelling effects, adopting parents' or other carers' anxiety-specific beliefs and avoidant behaviours.

Interventions

Biological approaches prescribe drugs such as benzodiazepines and tricyclic anti-depressants (clomipramine and imipramine). Tricyclic anti-depressants can have cardiac and electrocardiographically serious side-effects. SSRIs are also used and can also have some adverse side-effects.

Behavioural approaches include stimulus control, imaginal and *in vivo* systematic desensitisation, gradual exposure with relaxation training, modelling and rehearsal, operant conditioning (reward systems) and monitoring.

Cognitive approaches include psychoeducation, cognitive restructuring that is reappraisal and reattribution training along with breathing retraining, relaxation training, self-instructional skills and monitoring.

Eating disorders

Eating disorders include anorexia and bulimia. The peak age for onset is around the middle of adolescence. In adolescence eating disorders are characterised by an excessive preoccupation with body weight and shape. There is a refusal to maintain weight, an intense fear of gaining weight or being obese and excessive concern over size and shape, particularly the stomach, buttocks and thighs. Bulimia is recurrent binge-eating along with behaviour to prevent weight gain through purging and non-purging methods, e.g. vomiting, laxatives, diuretics and fasting and exercise. Physical complications may occur when adolescents develop eating disorders, such as amenorrhoea, delayed puberty, anaemia and electrolyte abnormalities. Anorexia and bulimia are most frequently seen among female adolescents. Other aspects include easy access to food, loss of personal and social interests, perfectionist attitudes, academic challenges and failure, depression and family conflict. There has been an increase in both disorders in Western countries and it is also increasing in non-Western countries. Eating disorders have a relatively high mortality rate, the highest for any psychological disorder.

Approaches

Biological approaches see eating disorders as due to a genetic predisposition and their maintenance as due to the neuroendocrine abnormalities that occur along with starvation.

Developmental theories see lifecycle transitions as contributing to eating disorders. Adolescents experience difficulties coping with the challenge of physical and emotional changes and develop a eating disorder as a coping mechanism.

Psychoanalytical approaches include seeing the over-controlling parenting style of mothers of anorexic girls as significant along with adolescent attempts to cope with conflicts surrounding independence and autonomy. Loss of a parent through bereavement and childhood sexual abuse are also contributory factors.

Behavioural approaches see positive reinforcement and negative reinforcement factors playing a part in maintaining anorexic behaviour. Anorexics feel positively reinforced through achieving control over their weight and negatively reinforced by avoiding criticisms of being overweight.

Cognitive approaches focus on cognitive distortions or errors in thinking that maintain excessive dieting and weight loss.

Family systems approaches regard family characteristics such as enmeshed, rigid families with overprotective parents and conflict avoidance as contributory to eating disorders although they could also be the consequences of family attempts to cope with adolescent eating problems. Other factors include fears about separation and abandonment.

Social approaches emphasise the cultural factors in Western countries that promote or idealise thinness as a highly desirable attribute for females.

Interventions

Severe cases require hospitalisation and family-based treatment. Family-based treatment aims to encourage a family culture where the adolescent is expected to revert to a normal eating routine or habit with parental support. The adolescent is trained to identify triggers for the binge–purge cycle. Finally, the family is encouraged to think of ways in which they can help the adolescent to achieve independence and privacy within the family. Problem-solving and communication skills training may be added as an adjunct to this approach.

Cognitive approaches aim through cognitive restructuring to challenge cognitive distortions and self-destructive attitudes and beliefs towards weight and shape. This approach includes psychoeducation and self-monitoring procedures.

Autism

Autism is the most common of the pervasive developmental disorders. These disorders are characterised by severe difficulties in social interaction, communication, language development and symbolic play. Any play they engage in tends to be repetitive and restricted. More males than females are autistic.

Asperger's syndrome is a form of autism characterised by severe difficulties in social interaction and repetitive and restricted play; however, unlike autism there are no difficulties in language and intellectual development. Autism appears in childhood and problems appear before the age of 3 years. Learning difficulties are apparent in most cases.

Autism is also characterised by Wing's triad – severe deficits in social development, language and behaviour. There is a lack of social reciprocity, a lack of secure attachment and a lack of empathy. Language development is delayed and there are speech abnormalities. Cognitively many autistic children have IQs below 70. However, some children have isolated abilities such as a good memory for facts. Behaviour is stereotypical, repetitive and restricted. There is also a strong drive to maintain routines and a resistance to change. They become isolated and often play on their own. Some children experience epilepsy, some develop encopresis and enuresis and some develop self-injurious behaviour such as head-banging. Some also develop behavioural problems such as aggressiveness and hyperactivity. The cause of autism is not known but there can be connections with other disorders such as congenital rubella, tuberous sclerosis and fragile X.

Autistic-like conditions are referred to as being along a continuum, the autistic spectrum. During adolescence deterioration can occur, often due to the onset of seizures. Autistic adolescents may find it difficult to cope with sexual desires or the changing demands of adolescence.

Approaches

Biological approaches consider genetic factors to be influential in the development of autism.

Cognitive approaches see cognitive deficits as being at the core of autism, these being a lack of social understanding, a lack a 'theory of mind' and a lack of an episodic autobiographical memory. Additionally it has been suggested that there is a problem with information-processing or in problem-solving.

Psychodynamic approaches propose cold, inadequate parents as being responsible for the characteristics of their autistic children. This theory does not have an empirical basis.

Interventions

There are currently no cures for autism. Early intervention is essential.

Biological approaches: there are no physical cures although drugs have been prescribed for some behavioural aspects of the condition, such as haloperidol and naltrexone.

Behavioural approaches include behaviour modification programmes based on operant conditioning that take place in the home and the school context. Behaviour modification programmes often include parent training. Sibling training has also been developed. These approaches stress that the child's environment should be structured and organised.

Anti-social behaviour (delinquency and other forms)

Anti-social behaviour occurs outside and within the law as some anti-social acts are committed by those under the age of criminal responsibility (age 10 in England and Wales and age 8 in Scotland and Northern Ireland). The legal definition of anti-social behaviour is that included in the Crime and Disorder Act 1998 and states that it is any behaviour that is likely to cause harassment, harm or distress to other people who are not in the same household as the one committing the offence. The types of anti-social behaviour include graffiti, abusive and threatening language, excessive noise, littering the streets, drunken behaviour and drug dealing. Types of adolescent anti-social behaviour include theft, truancy, vandalism, graffiti, arson, drug-taking and dealing. Murder is rare.

Most youth offending is theft-related and most offenders are male who commit 80 per cent of offences. However, the sex ratio of males to females is narrowing. It is common for adolescents to engage in unlawful behaviour at some point in their lives, e.g. drug-taking and petty theft. A significant minority, about a third, will go on to acquire a criminal record, particularly boys. Offending usually begins at around 14, lasts about 10 years, peaks at 18 for males and 15 for females and ends at 26. An early age of onset implies a consistent level of offending behaviour whereas some offending is limited to adolescence. Serious and persistent anti-social behaviour is noticeable as early as 3 years of age. A relatively small number of young repeat offenders (recidivists) are seen as responsible for a disproportionate amount of crime.

Psychological factors

Anti-social behaviour is associated with hyperactivity (restless, unsettled behaviour), cognitive impairment (poor reasoning and planning skills), temperament (impulsivity, risk-taking, sensation-seeking, aggressiveness and lack of self-control) and cognitive distortions (misinterpreting others' behaviour as hostile).

Social and family factors

Anti-social behaviour is associated with family conflict, parental abuse and neglect, inadequate parental supervision, poor parenting skills in particular coercive parenting, participation in deviant peer groups, social deprivation and disadvantage, unstable work histories and unemployment.

Prevention and intervention

Youth Justice System

Young offenders (10–18 years of age) under a new system can, if they admit their guilt, now receive an official 'reprimand' or a more serious 'warning'. Offenders who are warned are referred to a local authority multi-agency Youth Offending Team (YOT) who assess offenders' suitability for a rehabilitation programme and who may then implement it. Young people under 18 cannot be imprisoned but may be the subject of a detention and training order (DTO) for a period of between 4 months and 2 years consisting of attendance at a young offender institution (age 15 to 17) or secure training centre for those under 15 and supervision in the community. Young people under 18 can be the subject of supervision orders where they are supervised by probation officers, social workers or youth justice workers from the YOT. Young offenders up to the age of 20 can also receive an attendance centre order that requires supervised attendance on Saturday afternoons. Other measures include Youth Offender Panels (youth offender contract), curfews and electronic monitoring.

Young adult offenders (18–21) are cautioned and are tried in magistrates' and Crown courts.

Systems management includes decarceration (reducing/abolishing custodial sentences), diversion (reprimanding/warning offenders, Youth Offender Panels, Reparation Orders and Action Plan Orders, Anti-Social Behaviour Orders (ASBOs), acceptable behaviour contracts and inter-agency co-operation).

Psychological approaches

Cognitive-behavioural approaches to young offenders include:

- behavioural methods (contingency management, family-based behaviour modification, family contracting, individualised behaviour contracts);
- social skills training (modelling, guided group discussions, negotiation training, assertiveness training and anger management/replacement training);
- self-instructional training (self-control training, cognitive restructuring and problem-solving training);
- moral reasoning training;
- multi-modal (cognitive skills training, aggression replacement training and cognitive-behavioural programmes).

Parent management training (PMT) is based on the theory that parents of children with anti-social behaviour fail to reinforce appropriate pro-social behaviour while at the same time harshly punishing anti-social behaviour. As a consequence parents are likely to maintain their children's anti-social behaviour. PMT programmes are used to modify parents' behaviour during interactions with their children. These programmes include rule-setting, positively reinforcing pro-social behaviour (rewards, token economies), drawing up behaviour contracts and the use of mild punishments (time-out, withdrawal of privileges). Parents are trained to identify problem behaviours and to apply behavioural methods. PMT is more effective if combined with problem-solving training for the children. This approach requires motivated parents who understand the approach and is not applicable to those families who have a multiplicity of severe problems.

CHAPTER 5

Detailed topics

Adolescent aggressive behaviour

The concept

Aggressive behaviour is the outward manifestation of hostility towards others and the desire and intention to harm others. In its extreme form it becomes a conduct disorder.

Conduct disorders are attributed to adolescents where they manifest pervasive and persistent anti-social behaviour that occurs in the contexts of family, school and community. Such adolescents engage in the persistent breaking of rules, risk-taking, defiance of authority, destructiveness, deceitfulness and cruelty. They are frequently angry, irritable and impulsive and are often in conflict with their peers, parents and teachers. Theft, truancy and vandalism are other manifestations along with conflict with the police and involvement with social services and the youth justice system. This disorder is more prevalent in boys than girls and conduct disorders frequently co-occur with emotional disorders such as depression and anxiety. Different forms of adolescent aggression include defensive aggression (the intention is solely to defend oneself against attack), instrumental aggression (to achieve an aim with regard to other people or property), under-socialised (expressed by a solitary individual) and socialised (expressed by an individual who maintains social attachments).

- Identification of an aggressive act can vary depending on personal beliefs and social and cultural norms.
- Aggressive behaviour is manifested in varying degrees and can be seen as either categorical or dimensional, a trait or a state.
- Aggression is relatively common in adolescence, it can have its onset in early childhood or in adolescence and can persist into adulthood.
- If observable from an early age, then aggression tends to be stable through time.
- Males are more aggressive than females, ratio of 4:1.

Types

- physical or verbal: aggression using physical violence or verbal abuse;
- instrumental: the intention is to acquire an object, territory or privileges;
- emotional or expressive: the intention is to harm or injure another person.

Particular manifestations of adolescent aggressive behaviour

- Aggressive behaviour may take the form of physical and verbal aggression, bullying and cruelty towards peers. Adolescents may be hostile, defiant and rude towards adults. Lying, theft, violence, truancy, vandalism, substance abuse and fire-setting may occur.
- There may be difficulties with developing and maintaining peer relationships, or friendships may develop with younger or older peers.
- There is often egocentric and egoistic behaviour – manipulating others and being unconcerned about another's feelings or wishes.

Characteristics of adolescents with persistent and pervasive aggressive behaviour or conduct disorders

- There is a noticeable tendency to externalise guilt and tension, to blame others and to see others as hostile (a hostile attribution bias).
- There is often evidence of poor frustration tolerance, irritability, oppositional, provocative and unpredictable behaviour.
- There is also evidence of involvement in bullying, theft, vandalism and cruelty.
- There is often peer rejection, difficulties with peer relationships and low self-esteem but there can also be friendships with younger or older children, with individual delinquents and with gangs.
- There is some overlap with attention-deficit hyperactivity disorder (ADHD), substance abuse, learning difficulties, dyslexia and school under-achievement.

Theories of adolescent aggressive behaviour

There are a number of distinct theories but there is often a plurality of causes (multi-factorial) for aggressive behaviour.

Psychodynamic

Aggression is seen as an innate drive or predisposition that needs to be directed into socially acceptable channels. Early experiences of neglect, abandonment, abuse or stress are said to adversely affect an adolescent's self-control and adaptation to social norms. Adolescents who behave aggressively do so in order to protect themselves from the psychological pain arising from unconscious conflicts. They lack effective coping strategies to deal with these unpleasant feelings and instead resort to 'acting out' their feelings through aggressive, impulsive and delinquent behaviour. This aggressive behaviour in turn evokes negative responses which further exacerbate unpleasant feelings. They then rationalise their behaviour, believing their actions are reasonable and not socially deviant.

Aggression can also be seen as an outcome of insecure attachment and, as a result, adolescents have not grown up with an internal working model of a secure, trusting relationship.

Social learning

Aggression is seen as being the result of learning processes, i.e. modelling or reinforcement.

Children and adolescents are said to become aggressive and maintain aggressive behaviour through:

- observation of aggressive models, e.g. parents, peers and on TV;
- imitating those people who appear to gain rewards or reinforcement from their aggressive behaviour;
- being aggressive and receiving no punishment for it or receiving rewards or reinforcement for their aggression;
- receiving punishment and seeing it as a means of controlling others or getting their own way;
- self-justifying thought processes, e.g. attributing blame to others or claiming others deserve it.

Cognitive

Aggression is seen as the result of how children and adolescents come to perceive and understand behaviour and therefore is dependent on cognitive development, particularly cognitive appraisal. Aggressive adolescents frequently fail to detect positive or unintentional behaviours and they are often biased towards making attributions of aggression to others or blaming others.

Child-rearing and parenting practices

Aggression is seen as resulting from inadequate child-rearing and coercive parenting practices.

Parents engage in such practices, in part due to marital conflict, social and economic pressures, social isolation and the way they themselves were parented. Coercive parenting uses sanctions rather than praise and sanctions are harsh, inconsistent and often ineffective.

Children who experience parental conflict, physical or sexual abuse and emotional neglect are at risk of becoming aggressive adolescents as are those who have parents who engage in criminal activity or who are substance abusers.

Adolescent aggressive behaviour is also associated with parents who frequently use harsh, inconsistent and authoritarian discipline, corporal punishment and emotional humiliation.

Social skills and problem-solving skills deficit

Aggression is seen as due to a lack of social and problem-solving skills that are necessary for positive social and interpersonal interactions. There is a failure to consider alternative non-aggressive solutions to problems and a rapid resort to aggression.

Systems theory

Aggression is seen as the outcome of a disorganised family; roles, rules and routines are lacking or are absent or inconsistent. There is poor communication; a lack of empathy and a state of confusion and disorder. There is also a lack of problem-solving skills when it comes to resolving family disputes.

Aggression can also be seen as multi-systemic in that several systems contribute to aggressive behaviour namely:

- the individual (temperament, learning difficulties, poor social skills)
- the family (family disorganisation, coercive parenting)
- the school (punitive discipline)
- the community (deviant peer group and poor neighbourhood)

Neurological

ADHD and conduct disorders frequently overlap.

Assessment

Assessment of aggressive adolescents should be based on a multi-modal approach, i.e. drawing information from different sources and using a number of assessment methods.

Imprecise labels such as 'aggressive' and 'hostile' should be avoided and be replaced by terms or phrases that are more specific and informative.

A **history** of the adolescent's childhood behaviour should be obtained along with any relevant medical conditions.

Interviewing should elicit:

- an adolescent's personal experience and understanding of aggression;
- any antecedents and consequences that serve to trigger aggression;
- any cognitive distortion, e.g. misinterpreting other people's behaviour as suspicious or aggressive;
- any cognitive deficit, e.g. having inadequate problem-solving skills.

Self-monitoring is where adolescents are asked to monitor aggressive incidents along with their antecedents and consequences through using an 'anger log'. This can also be used to record contexts, time, people present and adolescents' views of the incidents.

Direct observation is where an observer observes the adolescent's behaviour in the various contexts where the aggressive behaviour occurs and records it according to its antecedents and consequences and its latency, frequency and duration.

Formulation

Formulation is the summarising and interpreting of assessment information in a way that enables hypotheses to be generated. The formulation specifies the factors that appear to trigger and maintain the identified behaviour. The aim is to identify the contingencies that maintain a particular behaviour, a functional or ABC analysis being useful in this regard.

Interventions

To be effective, interventions should be appropriate to the context and appropriate for the person implementing the intervention.

Behavioural approaches

Positive reinforcement is used to reinforce non-aggressive behaviour, which can take the form of positive attention, or non-material (praise) or material rewards.

Time-out involves removing adolescents from rewarding situations for aggressive behaviour; this includes removing reinforcers from the adolescent or removing the adolescent from the reinforcing context or situation.

Token economies or **behavioural contracts** enable adolescents to earn tokens for non-aggressive behaviours, which may be exchanged immediately or saved. Tokens can be exchanged for privileges or material goods.

Assertiveness training involves training adolescents to assert themselves non-aggressively in order to achieve their rights.

Another strategy is teaching parents **behavioural interventions** and encouraging parents to apply them in the home.

Cognitive and social learning

Modelling is where an adult role model demonstrates non-aggressive or assertiveness alternatives to the use of aggressive behaviour in attaining legitimate goals.

Self-instructional training is where an adult encourages an adolescent to monitor the thoughts that contribute to aggressive behaviour and to substitute self-statements that reduce or extinguish aggressive responses. Adolescents are asked to think non-aggressively when they are aware of events that normally lead to aggressive acts.

Problem-solving training is where an adult proposes an alternative model to trying to solve problems through aggression. Using this model an adolescent is encouraged to go through stages that include defining the problem, identifying aggressive thinking, setting goals, thinking of alternatives to aggressive solutions, implementing the alternative solutions and evaluating outcomes.

Anger control is where adolescents are taught to recognise, monitor and control anger (emotional arousal) and the accompanying aggression. However, it must be remembered that not all anger results in aggression. Hostile attributional style also plays a part in fuelling anger and aggressiveness. In order to control their anger, adolescents are asked to identify the behavioural, physiological and cognitive elements of their anger and to monitor events and situations that trigger anger through using an anger log or diary and an anger thermometer. Containment of anger is aided through adolescents applying coping self-statements and reattributing blame.

Cognitive-based forms of training can be made more effective through combining them with behavioural techniques, e.g. positive reinforcement and relaxation training.

Attention-deficit hyperactivity disorder (ADHD)

The concept

ADHD as a diagnosis is more prevalent in the USA (from 2 per cent to 10 per cent of children) than in the UK but currently it is attracting more attention in the UK. It is usually a condition of childhood and early adolescence.

It is diagnosed using either the DSM-IV criteria, or the ICD-10 criteria, by a doctor or a psychiatrist. Prevalence rates vary according to different criteria and to the strictness of the criteria adopted. There may be over-inclusion or under-inclusion of children as having ADHD. Boys outnumber girls.

The main symptoms are: inattention, hyperactivity and impulsivity and these symptoms should have persisted for at least six months, be manifested in two settings and have had an onset before the age of 7 years and not be the result of some other mental disorder, brain injury or physical condition.

There are various categories within ADHD – namely children who are mainly **inattentive** or **hyperactive-impulsive**, or both. Conduct disorders, enuresis and learning difficulties overlap with ADHD. Peer rejection also occurs. Some children do outgrow the disorder. In adolescence, children with ADHD have an increased risk of delinquency, truancy, substance abuse and difficulties with relationships.

Causes

attention	There appears to be no defect as it were with a child's attentional mechanisms; however, such children have difficulty paying attention where there are large gaps between the presentation of tasks. They cannot bear waiting for long and act impulsively. The problem seems more to do with self-regulation of behaviour.
heredity	There appears to be some genetic influence.

| **neurotransmitters** | Hyperactivity does appear to be connected to neurotransmitter activity, e.g. that of dopamine and norepinephrine. |
| **home background** | Parenting practices and stressors in the home can contribute to school difficulties. |

Assessment

A multi-method assessment approach is recommended using information from parents and teachers and observations of the child across different settings. Evidence for ADHD is required in terms of an early age of onset, persistence and its occurrence across several settings. Some forms of assessment might discriminate against ethnic minorities through over-inclusion.

Interventions

Behavioural (operant conditioning techniques)

Positive reinforcement involves both parents and teachers reinforcing on-task behaviour. This approach also requires parents and teachers to identify the antecedents and consequences of inattention, impulsivity and hyperactivity and where possible manipulate the antecedents and consequences of those behaviours.

Response cost and time-out strategies can also be used. Response cost occurs where a child receives a penalty or sanction for engaging in inappropriate behaviour. Time-out is time out from positive reinforcement (e.g. teacher and peer attention) which can mean being placed outside a classroom or sent to bed for non-compliance.

An optimal behavioural intervention would combine positive reinforcement with response cost and time-out.

Cognitive

Self-monitoring involves children attending to and recording their own behaviour. Self-reinforcement requires children to monitor and reinforce their own behaviour, this being combined with reinforcement provided by teachers and parents.

Medication

This requires the administering of psychostimulant drugs to children, the most common being methylphenidate (Ritalin). Tricyclic anti-depressants have also been prescribed.

Stimulants act to increase attention and alertness through their action on the brain. These drugs are effective with 70 per cent to 80 per cent of primary school-children, although there are lower rates of effectiveness with adolescents, i.e. 50 per cent to 70 per cent. However, long-term effectiveness of the stimulants remains in question. The effect of the stimulant drug is to increase attention span and to reduce disruption both in the home and in the classroom. There can be side-effects, e.g. sleep problems, reduced appetite, headaches and stomach-aches and tics. In the long term, height and weight gain can be suppressed but with termination of medication, growth returns.

There is a danger that if over-inclusion occurs, then children not suffering from ADHD will have the stimulant prescribed. It should be noted that children receiving the stimulant who do not manifest ADHD also experience an increase in attention span and alertness.

It is often recommended that the intervention approach to ADHD should be multi-modal, meaning that there should be a combination of different types of intervention, e.g. medication along with behavioural-type strategies. Furthermore, it is often stated that claims of curing ADHD should be approached with caution.

Parents and teachers and ADHD

Teachers and parents, by using interventions like those listed below, can help the child with ADHD.

Behavioural approaches

These are based on behaviour management using operant techniques, e.g. positive reinforcement and sanctions – response cost and time-out. Response cost is where a loss of positive reinforcement occurs if inappropriate behaviour is displayed. Time-out involves withdrawing all reinforcers for a stipulated brief period of time depending on behaviour. There is no access to reinforcers during that time.

Rewards should be given frequently and immediately after the desired behaviours are performed. Sanctions should be coupled with rewards and similarly be specific and immediately implemented after the inappropriate behaviour.

Social skills training can help through the use of modelling, behavioural rehearsal and anger management.

Work should be varied and broken down into small tasks and steps.

Cognitive approaches

Adolescents can be encouraged to monitor their own behaviour as a way of increasing their attention to tasks.

They can also be trained to evaluate their behaviour and then reward appropriate behaviours.

Adolescent depression

The concept of depression

It has become accepted that depressive states resembling adult depression can and do appear in childhood. Depression is not rare but is more frequent in adolescence than in childhood. It is more common among adolescent girls than boys.

The categories used to classify and distinguish different sorts of depression are: unipolar and bipolar mood disorders, severe episodic disorders and milder, more persistent forms of depression. These are in turn distinguished from disorders that are secondary to medical conditions. Depression can occur along with (co-morbidity) other disorders such as anxiety, conduct and attention deficit disorders.

Symptoms

The symptoms for major depression are:

- depressed or irritable mood most of the day;
- loss of interest or pleasure;
- failure to gain expected weight;
- insomnia or excessive sleep;
- agitation or loss of energy;
- feelings of worthlessness or inappropriate guilt;
- a sense of hopelessness;
- poor concentration;
- persistent thoughts of suicide;
- delusions and hallucinations may also occur – delusions focusing on guilt, illness, death, punishment, personal inadequacy and persecution, and hallucinatory thoughts having an abusive or suicidal content.

To be diagnosed as having a major depression, an adolescent must experience five or more of the above symptoms for the same two-week period. There is some overlap with other problems, e.g. separation anxiety, school refusal, anti-social behaviour, substance abuse, anorexia and physical complaints.

With adolescents there may be additional symptoms, e.g. delinquency, use of drugs, moodiness, restlessness, reluctance to participate in family and social occasions and difficulties at school or college.

There is an increase in depressive feelings with age, particularly comparing adolescence with pre-adolescence. Depression is found to be higher among adolescent girls than boys. There is evidence that the prevalence of depression is increasing among adolescents. Most adolescents recover from depression within a year but are likely to develop depression later in adulthood.

Parents and teachers may be unaware of an adolescent's suicidal ideas and feelings; this is because adolescents may not 'act out' their feelings and so are overlooked.

Causes of depression

All episodes of depression are generally seen as reactive in the sense that they are preceded by stressful triggers.

Predisposing and precipitating factors:

parental depression	A depressed adolescent may have depressed parents or relatives or parents experiencing some other psychiatric problem that contributes to the adolescent's depression.
poor interpersonal relationships	depressed adolescents may experience negative relationships with their parents (particularly rejection), siblings and their peers.
bereavement	Premature parental death along with other kinds of bereavement precipitates depression among children and adolescents. Such bereavement may result in an adolescent feeling guilt, low self-esteem and gloominess about the future. There may also be internalising of behavioural problems. Shock occurs and as a result there may be denial and disbelief, hallucinations, anger, despair and hopelessness. Delinquency, drug and alcohol abuse, school refusal and refusal to engage with school or college work are other symptoms that may manifest themselves.
divorce and marital conflict	These may result in an adolescent experiencing severe depression.
physical and sexual abuse	Where adolescents experience physical or sexual abuse they are at risk of becoming depressed and may also manifest other problems, e.g. anxiety, guilt, shame and aggression.

Approaches

Behavioural approach

Operant conditioning (Skinner): a lack of or a low level of positive reinforcement of an individual's responses may lead to that individual feeling depressed and can be further exacerbated by the individual not having the necessary social skills to obtain rewards.

Cognitive-behavioural approaches

Learned-helplessness is where individuals have learned to have expectations that events are beyond their control and that the inevitable result will be unpleasant consequences. These expectations lead the individual to become resigned to these consequences and not attempt to reassert control over the situation.

Attributional style can lead to depression where an individual attributes his or her failure to achieve goals due to a combination of internal, stable and global causes, e.g. if one attributes a failure in one's relationships to one's inadequate personality. This attributional style may result from negative parental criticism being internalised and thus lead the adolescent to engage in excessive self-criticism.

Depressogenic (depression-producing cognitions) schema (Beck, 1976) can lead to depression where individuals come to have a pessimistic view of themselves, the world and the future. Individuals who persistently interpret their experiences negatively tend to become depressed.

Adolescents who have cognitive distortions tend to experience lower self-esteem, hopelessness and are less able to recall positive events. Adolescents frequently make social comparisons between themselves and their peers and if as a result they constantly receive negative feedback, they may develop a negative self-schema that predisposes them to depression.

Problem-solving skills deficit: depression is seen as being maintained by a lack of positive reinforcement and by the absence or lack of the necessary problem-solving skills that are needed to acquire positive reinforcement.

Family systems approach: depressed adolescents frequently come from families where there are high rates of depression or other disorders. These adolescents may mirror the depression of their parents. Parental rejection can have an important bearing on an adolescent's depression.

Interventions

Cognitive-behavioural (individual or group-based)

- **Self-monitoring**: involves asking the adolescent to attend to and record his or her own thoughts and feelings. This activity can be seen as both a means of assessment and form of therapy. Self-monitoring by the adolescent of positive events may lead to the adolescent increasing his or her sensitivity and awareness for positive events.

- **Self-evaluation training**: involves changing the way adolescents consider themselves so that they evaluate themselves more positively.

- **Cognitive restructuring**: involves challenging an adolescent's negative way of thinking along with its underlying assumptions. Evidence is sought for the adolescent's negative beliefs. Alternative interpretations of a depressing event are also generated along with the possibility of more positive outcomes.

- **Self-reinforcement**: occurs where adolescents are asked to reward themselves for thinking and behaving more positively.

Social skills training

Various procedures are used to teach depressed adolescents social skills including modelling, role play, positive reinforcement and feedback.

Problem-solving skills training

Adolescents are encouraged to proceed through a problem-solving skills staged approach in order to increase positive reinforcement. Positive reinforcement is planned for through a programme of pleasant activities and positive social interactions. This staged approach comprises defining the problem, considering alternative solutions, implementing the most practical of these solutions and then evaluating the outcome.

Family systems approach

The aim is to empower family members to help adolescents control their moods by challenging their depressive thoughts and feelings and to encourage adolescents to engage in positive interactions with other members of the family.

Psychodynamic approach

Psychodynamic psychotherapy aims to help adolescents to achieve insight into their depression through interpreting and working through defences used in past and present relationships.

Suicide and attempted suicide

The concepts

Suicide is the taking of one's life and its criminal status as self-murder did not end until 1961. Suicide is closely connected to having a psychiatric illness such as a major depression, alcoholism, schizophrenia or a personality disorder, in particular, a borderline or an anti-social personality disorder. It is a leading cause of death among adolescents and has risen sharply since the 1960s, particularly among young working-class males, those 15 to 24 since 1982, and there is a higher rate of suicide among young males as against females, a current ratio of 6:1. Adolescents who commit suicide tend to display a combination of depression along with a conduct disorder. The risk increases rapidly through adolescence and into the early adult years. There is a higher rate among young Asian females compared to their white female counterparts. There is also a high rate of depression and suicide among the young unemployed and young males in remand centres and among murderers. There is also a higher rate for those suffering physical illnesses such as epilepsy, temporal-lobe epilepsy, Huntington's chorea, cancer, multiple sclerosis and AIDS. Methods mostly used are hanging, car exhausts and overdosing. Males tend to use more lethal methods than females.

Attempted suicide or parasuicide is far commoner among females than males, increasing among girls from 12 years upwards and peaking at 16 years of age. The general rate has been increasing since 1990 and in particular there has been a rise in the male rate. In fact, having suicidal thoughts is not that rare.

Suicidal thinking

Particular thoughts and motives may occur in an adolescent's suicidal thought processes:

- that one will be reunited with a loved one or will be reborn;
- that one will escape despair and attain a state of tranquillity;
- self-punishment and punishment of others or revenge;
- an appeal for help by expressing intentions beforehand;
- a sense of control over an intolerable situation;
- frequent hints or talk of suicide indicate that the suicidal process is accelerating;

- persistent angry and severe suicidal thoughts tend to lead to repeated attempts;
- poor problem-solving thought processes;
- feeling trapped by circumstances or by thoughts and feelings.

Causes

Predisposing causes:

- experiencing unemployment that results in poverty, social isolation, disengagement from the community, loss of self-esteem and identity;
- having lost a parent in childhood or having a parent who suffers from psychiatric problems, physical health problems, alcoholism or domestic violence;
- parental emotional, physical or sexual abuse;
- combination of parental rejection and overprotectiveness;
- parental divorce and separation;
- regular bullying at school, problems with school work and with teachers;
- depression;
- schizophrenia;
- alcohol and substance abuse.

Precipitating causes:

- loss or separation, e.g. breaking up with a boyfriend or girlfriend or experiencing a bereavement;
- modelling others' suicidal behaviours, i.e. having peers or relatives who have attempted or died through suicide or even imitating suicides reported in the media;
- arguments with a partner, parent, relatives or a boyfriend;
- a stressful work or financial situation;
- exam failure.

Approaches

Psychodynamic approaches

Freudians see individuals who are over-dependent on significant others for their own positive sense of self as likely to find the loss of others as unbearable. Reproach of the loss is not possible therefore self-reproach occurs, leading ultimately to an urge for self-destruction. Others have stressed aggressive impulses.

Bowlby focuses on insecure attachment. Individuals become fearful of abandonment and loneliness and end up in a state of self-contempt and rage. Suicidal behaviour then becomes a way of securing attachment by signalling distress to others or alternatively becomes a means of punishing others' rejection.

Cognitive approaches

Cognitive distortions are seen as playing a part in precipitating depression and in certain cases leading ultimately to suicide. A depressogenic schema is a filter that biases towards negative information processing and thereby leads to feelings of hopelessness and personal inadequacy. Memory becomes biased towards negative events and retrieval of positive events is reduced. Problem-solving is also reduced and the approach to problems is predominantly generalised rather than specific.

Social comparison is a means of judging one's appearance, rank, status and achievement in relation to that of others. Self-esteem is based on social comparison. Where social comparison is unfavourable, that is where there is a perceived failure in achieving or maintaining one's relative status, then depression may be the consequence.

Biological approaches

Depression is seen as being connected to neurotransmitter depletion. In the case of suicide, serotonin is seen as a major factor. As regards genetic factors, a multiple gene effect might be involved as a risk factor in suicide but one that requires an environmental trigger.

Prevention and interventions

Depression sometimes goes unrecognised by GPs for various reasons and ends up untreated. Therefore, vigilance is needed for verbal or mood cues. Prevention of suicide can be achieved through the reduction of lethal methods, e.g. detoxification of domestic gas or prescription of non-toxic drugs. Samaritan centres provide active listeners for those who are depressed and those who are contemplating suicide. School-based intervention programmes focus on increasing awareness of suicide as a problem, provide information about available support and encourage at-risk adolescents to seek help.

With regard to interventions, counsellors need to be vigilant for verbal and mood cues that may indicate suicidal intentions. Expressed hopelessness is seen as a strong verbal cue as is a sudden change in mood. They also need to consider what methods are available, e.g. self-poisoning. Certain questions can be asked in order to help reveal how far suicide is being considered. These questions are whether people feel any hope, whether they have suicidal ideas or fantasies, whether they are planning suicide and whether it is soon and who else would be concerned over an attempt. Explicit discussion of reasons cited by the person is helpful in terms of addressing problems realistically and does not increase the likelihood of suicide. Counsellors need also to identify the resources available to people and their individual strengths. The aim is to provide people with a sense of control over their problems.

Cognitive-behavioural approaches

The focus is on challenging and changing cognitive distortions that contribute to depressive and suicidal states of mind or on enabling the person to acquire problem-solving skills that ameliorate those states.

Cognitive therapy addresses cognitive distortions such as:

- **dichotomous or either/or thinking**: thinking that there is no middle way of solving a problem;
- **selective abstraction**: focusing on some aspects of a problem to the exclusion of others;
- **arbitrary inference**: a problematic conclusion is drawn from unrelated evidence;
- **over-generalisation**: concluding that one negative event will inevitably be followed by others;
- **catastrophising**: thinking that this is the worst possible situation one could face.

Problem-solving skills therapy encourages people to believe they can control their thoughts and feelings and provides them with skills to address their problems. It proceeds through stages that encourage problem definition and analysis and the generation of alternative solutions, the pros and cons and outcomes of those solutions, testing those solutions through cognitive rehearsal and activity scheduling, using self-reinforcement to reward success and finally evaluating solutions.

Dialectical behaviour therapy combines cognitive-restructuring, problem-solving skills training and contingency management with person-centred counselling techniques. The dialectical aspect focuses on balancing acceptance of stressful events along with changing them.

Self-harm

The concept

People who self-harm inflict wounds on the body, often in a private, habitual and deliberate way. It is a behaviour that is usually found in adolescents, mainly in young women and in people in their twenties and thirties. There is a growing problem among young Asian women. Gay men and women also experience a disproportionately high rate of self-harm. It is also more prevalent among young people who have a learning disability. Young people are more vulnerable because they are more likely to live in abusive and unsupportive families, or they may be grappling with sexual orientation difficulties, learning difficulties and may not possess adequate coping skills. Self-harm may enable young people to experience a sense of control over their lives and some form of independence and self-identity. Its origin can often be traced to physically and sexually abusive experiences in childhood and to childhood neglect. Early losses, bereavements, and deaths of parents and siblings are also implicated. Self-harm can be seen as an alarming but comprehensible, meaningful behaviour that is amenable to rational explanation and intervention.

Both women and men self-harm by cutting their arms, thighs and stomachs or breasts. Usually the cutting is superficial but sometimes the wounds are deeper and leave scars. Sometimes self-harm takes the form of burns on the skin. At other times the person hits parts of the body, banging the head, slapping the face or punching walls. Other people scratch a wound and pick at it so that it remains a permanent sore.

Certain religious practices are associated with socially supported self-injury, such as forms of atonement, punishment and purification like self-flagellation. Self-injury is also associated with initiation rites of passage such as scarification and circumcision.

Self-harm is particularly prevalent in secure environments such as penal institutions, special hospitals, children's homes and hostels. The incidents often take place at night and in privacy. Each case seems to vary in frequency. Sometimes cutting takes place on a regular basis but often self-harm occurs when feelings cannot be managed and there can be weeks or months between incidents.

Approaches

Self-harming behaviour serves significant psychological functions, and there are a variety of psychological approaches.

Psychodynamic

Most people who self-harm seek to cope with unbearable feelings such as shame, guilt and unworthiness. Sometimes this may be caused by fear and shame about sexual arousal. Others see the healing after cutting as some sort of purging of mental and emotional distress. Some experience a sense of relief when the blood flows, and others confirm their aliveness at the sight of blood which as well as marking the skin can be seen as a symbolic manifestation of healing and salvation. Cutting the skin, which is a container of self and represents the boundary between the self and non-self, is a way of expressing deep distress; and for many people taking care of the skin after mutilation provides a kind of soothing.

Some people express their loss or grief through self-harming and others experience a sense of power and control. For others, it is an expression of despair, anger, frustration or protest. It can be seen as a means of self-punishment, a re-enactment of past traumatic and abusive events. Sometimes it is an indirect way of communicating something, or a way of punishing or manipulating another person.

Another explanation of self-harm is that it represents a partial suicide. It is a way of coping with aggression that cannot be expressed in any other way. Alternatively it is seen as a means of relieving guilt feelings associated with illicit activities or internal conflicts that have not been resolved. The internalised process of early object relationships and the early psychological pain resulting from loss and separation, feelings of abandonment, poor boundaries and enmeshed family relationships are contributory factors. Feelings of hopelessness, ambivalence, confusion, anxiety, lack of focus, poor relationships, depression, lack of self-esteem and lack of self-worth contribute to self-harming behaviour.

Cognitive-behavioural

Self-harming behaviour can be seen as an extreme reaction to loss or abandonment. This in turn leads to feelings of hopelessness, and the belief that current difficulties are unbearable and unmanageable. Self-harming people think that there are few alternatives to this behaviour. It is necessary to understand cognitive content of self-harming ideation and intentions. Many people who self-harm are not able to think of alternative options to cope with their problems; they possess 'cognitive rigidity'. They also have negative beliefs about the self, the world and the future.

People are more at risk of self-harming when they feel hungry, angry, lonely or tired. Other factors that make people vulnerable are acute and chronic pain or illness, substance abuse, or major life loss or major life change.

Interventions and treatment

Talking about self-harm can increase, decrease or have no effect on the likelihood of the self-harming behaviour, depending on the content and context of the discussion, the participants and the reaction of the young person. Yet it often helps the adolescent to know that someone is listening and understanding the self-harming behaviour. At least explicit discussion of self-harm makes it possible to address the issues directly and more likely to reduce the frequency of it.

Sometimes a referral to a psychiatrist might be desirable, especially if the young person has poor impulse and dysfunctional thoughts are such that suicidal ideation and suicidal plans are detected.

The therapist needs to work towards establishing rapport so that a collaborative and trusting relationship can develop where the patient feels supported and understood. The therapist needs to be available, reliable and resourceful. The boundaries must be clear and transparent. The patient needs to feel that the therapist is interested in his or her current situation and history but does not feel overwhelmed by the person's problems or self-harming behaviour.

Psychodynamic

The therapist needs to establish a relationship with the patient, establishing an empathic bond without the pitfalls of inappropriate attachment, where the patient demands love and avoids expressing vulnerability. The work with the patient can focus on despair and anxiety in the hope that the patient can see that through therapy it is possible to develop other options to cope with hopelessness apart from self-harming.

The cessation of the self-harming behaviour is not necessarily seen as a target for therapy, for the therapist's task is to help the patient explore the inner world and make meaning of the behaviour. One of the fundamental changes that can occur is for the patient to feel safe, so that, together, patient and therapist can examine the origin of the problem as well as the current situation. The self-harming behaviour, therefore, can be seen as a way of communicating something that is unresolved in the patient's inner world, in the way he or she uses the body and expresses him- or herself and relates to others, and as such it can help both participants comprehend something of the patient's pain, struggle and longing.

Working through the patient's unmanageable feelings, particularly anger, is important for therapeutic change or development. The therapist elicits the patient's angry feelings towards the parent, enabling the therapist to work with the transference. This can happen when the patient sees the therapist as if he or she behaves like the parental imagos (as if the therapist is the original parent figure that the patient has internalised). The therapist must be seen to survive the patient's destructive inner feelings and hatred through keeping to the boundaries and by interpreting the patient's feelings. The therapist's unexpressed counter-transference feelings become the material for making interpretations which therapeutically help to resolve the patient's inner conflicts.

Cognitive-behavioural

The aim of this approach is to provide the person with a more effective way of coping with problems. This can be achieved through cognitive restructuring of thoughts, behaviour and emotions. The focus should be in particular on the thoughts and feelings of hopelessness and despair. It can be helpful to get the patient to look carefully at the evidence that it is necessary to self-harm to achieve desired goals. This means looking at cognitive distortions surrounding the felt need to self-harm. It involves challenging those distortions and presenting alternatives. Furthermore, one should list the advantages and disadvantages of self-harm. This may raise self-doubt regarding the benefits of self-harm and also identify alternative behaviours. Having reached this point, agreement can be made on a course of action or a contract to refrain from self-harm during which time the therapist and the person can work to resolve the problems.

Other elements of this approach include **anger management**, where anger is a significant component of self-harm, and **self-management**, where impulse control is poor. It is often the case that alternative solutions to cutting become apparent as the work progresses even if these are not necessarily the primary choice of the patient. Many patients will be resistant to these alternative choices and work might be slow and painstaking.

Eating disorders

The concept

The main eating disorders are anorexia nervosa, bulimia and obesity.

Anorexia nervosa

The onset of this disorder is often in adolescence, increasing rapidly after 13 years of age, and at a maximum between the ages of 17 to 18 years. It is much more common in females than males, and it is on the increase. This eating disorder is where an adolescent, usually a teenage girl, although boys suffer from it too, has severe problems with body image and who as a result pursues thinness to the point of starvation.

The criteria for anorexia are:

- restricting food intake to the point of refusing to eat hardly anything at all;
- refusal to maintain body weight less than 85 per cent of normal for age;
- intense fear of gaining weight and becoming fat;
- distortion of image of body weight and shape;
- cessation of periods over three consecutive cycles.

Other symptoms of sufferers of the disorder:

- preoccupation with food;
- depression;
- denial of symptoms;
- resistance to treatment;
- suppression of sexual development;
- conflicts with parents.

Bulimia

Bulimia often occurs later in adolescence than anorexia, it is much more common than anorexia and is predominantly a female disorder.

This disorder is characterised by a fear of weight gain which leads to repeated bouts of binge eating, frequently followed by self-induced vomiting and purging, or the abuse of laxatives and diuretics. The bulimic's weight is just below normal, normal or even above normal.

The criteria for bulimia are:

- repeated sessions of binge eating;
- repeated sessions of purging through use of laxatives, diuretics and enemas in order to avoid weight gain;
- binge eating occurs at least twice a week over a period of three months;
- self-esteem is disproportionately influenced by concerns over body shape and weight.

Other characteristics of bulimia:

- depression;
- excessive exercise;
- feeling out of control;
- shoplifting;
- alcohol dependence;
- tends to appear after or during dieting or during episodes of anorexia;
- less resistant to treatment than anorexics.

Secondary conditions are often detected in both anorexia and bulimia sufferers, such as depression, anxiety, obsessive-compulsive behaviour, severe stress symptoms and substance abuse.

Obesity

Obesity occurs in female as well as male children and adolescents, and it occurs when the young person puts on excessive weight.

Obesity is usually defined in terms of body weight being anything between 15 per cent and 30 per cent of a person's ideal weight. Age, sex and height as well as different cultural attitudes are taken into consideration.

The criteria for obesity are:

- Food intake is excessive and uncontrolled.
- Food intake is of mainly fattening foods.
- The adolescent is suffering from a physical disorder.

Approaches

There are many approaches, and many books have been written on the subject of eating disorders. Two approaches that seem somewhat to explain the disorder are:

Psychodynamic

Anorexia arises from early childhood experiences. One theory asserts that the parenting style of mothers of anorexic girls emphasises control and compliance to mothers, thus the child's needs for self-expression and autonomy become secondary. The child has difficulty learning how to interpret need-related internal physiological states and in developing a coherent sense of self.

In adolescence the fear of fatness, obsession with food and guilt for eating are part of an attempt to manage a central conflict related to the attainment of autonomy and a coherent sense of self.

The youngster experiences a fear of separation from parents and a fear of being overtly controlled by the parents, as well as fear of maturation, sexuality, intimacy and independence and a fear of having little control over the self or body size (as a symbol of self).

This conflict about autonomy is characterised by negative self-evaluative beliefs (low self-esteem) coupled with perfectionist strivings to improve the self.

There is ample evidence of distorted perception of body image, maturity fears, perfectionist strivings, low self-esteem and low self-efficacy among teenagers with eating disorders.

Early stressful events, such as loss of a parent through bereavement and child sexual abuse, are more common among children and teenagers with eating disorders, particularly bulimia.

Therapy aims to help the patient gain insight into the way in which the psycho-dynamic past relationship with parents underpins the transference/counter-transference patient – therapist relationship and relationships with other significant people. In learning to develop a sense of self in the therapeutic relationship, the adolescent begins to learn autonomy and gain a more realistic body image.

Cognitive-behavioural

Particular settings, events and personal characteristics combine with particular triggering events to help predispose youngsters to perceiving restrictive eating as desirable behaviour.

Family-based difficulties that prevent the adolescent from being able to establish autonomy, as well as social anxiety in peer relationships, can result in eating problems.

Stressful events such as when the youngster has perfectionist strivings to be in control and achieve success predispose adolescents to eating disorders.

Some traumatic early experiences such as abuse or separation anxiety are some of the factors that can lead adolescents to abuse their bodies.

Criticism from peers and family may lead to dieting behaviour that gradually increases the risk of the adolescent developing eating problems.

When the adolescent loses weight, weight loss can be seen as a sign of success and the adolescent can feel in control of his or her body, which can then re-inforce the eating problem. Sometimes slightly overweight adolescents avoid criticism of their body size by losing weight, and thus begin a cycle of eating problems.

The obsession of society with body image reinforces the belief that being slim is more desirable, and adolescents strive to emulate models and pop stars and in so doing they can lose sight of what is healthy.

Assessment

Assessment can sometimes be difficult due to similarities in symptoms that anorexia and bulimia share. It is often useful first to develop a 'trusting' relationship with the adolescent before attempting to diagnose the severity of the problem due mainly to 'resistance'. The young person might not be emotionally aware and as a result he or she might find it difficult to address the issues that will help diagnosis. He or she might be resistant to opening themselves up and might find questions intrusive. Adolescents often find it difficult to talk to an adult about their bodies but most respond to sensitive and empathic clinicians who are non-judgemental, and are willing and able to listen to the adolescent's problems.

Methods used to diagnose anorexia and bulimia:

- **interviewing**, e.g. ascertaining facts about the adolescent's existing problems relating to food consumption, including 'forbidden foods', i.e. foods avoided and also the adolescent's weight history;

- **self-report inventories**, e.g. instruments designed to measure some aspects of eating disorders;

- **direct observation** of dietary restraint, i.e. those attitudes and behaviours that an adolescent adopts in order to lose weight;

- **accurate measurement of weight**: anorexics are well below normal weight whereas bulimics can be under, over or normal;

- **self-monitoring** of food consumption, e.g. revealing antecedent events leading to bingeing sessions;

- **measurement** of body image distortion.

Formulation

Psychodynamic approach

Anorexics are seen as having problems or conflicts in terms of individualising, in terms of gaining control over their lives and in forming a particular gender identity. They are seen as having particular difficulties in coping with the mature genital stage (adult sexuality) and as a result regress to an earlier stage. Or they are seen as striving to attain their own identity after being subservient to their mother's demands in the past.

Behavioural approach

Anorexia is seen as a result of maladaptive learning whereby, for example, an adolescent after frequent rows at mealtimes may come to associate eating with unpleasantness or where an adolescent refuses to eat and gains attention or where losing weight reduces teasing.

Cognitive approach

Anorexia is seen as a direct result of cognitive distortions regarding body weight. It is also seen as a form of avoidance behaviour, i.e. dieting, exercise and purgatives are used to avoid the perceived threat of obesity. The achievement of thinness is self-reinforcing in that it evokes a sense of self-control, which comes with dieting.

Treatment

It is important for adolescents to have access to information on what constitutes healthy eating and how easy it is for teenagers to develop eating problems. Sometimes adolescents cope better with eating problems when they are able to join a self-help group or a peer group where issues related to food can be discussed openly and they can share experiences and encourage each other to eat healthily.

It helps adolescents to discuss eating problems directly and in detail with parents, teachers, doctor or other significant adults including counsellors and therapists.

Adolescents benefit from individual treatment plans to improve eating behaviour. The plan needs to incorporate the following:

- regular eating;
- varied nutrition;
- avoiding diet products;
- avoiding filling stomach with fluid;
- eating in the company of others;
- keeping a journal.

Apart from helping the adolescent with an eating programme, counsellors, therapists and parents can further help the young person distinguish self-esteem and self-acceptance from physical appearance. Counsellors and therapists need to take the adolescent's feelings of guilt or shame into account, and challenge dysfunctional thoughts. In so doing they can help the young person search for less destructive ways to assert autonomy from the parents and develop a strong sense of personal identity.

The treatment of anorexia and bulimia is often multi-modal, meaning that various approaches are used, e.g. individual psychotherapy, behavioural and cognitive-behavioural.

Psychodynamic therapy: This approach is helpful because it addresses the anorexic's resistances, particularly as anorexia is a core identity for many adolescents with the disorder. In the relationship with the therapist the adolescent can slowly begin to build a sense of self through the exploration of the many unmanageable and unresolved anxieties that are hidden from the conscious mind of the young person.

Behavioural therapy: The main approach is positive reinforcement (praise and attention) of appropriate behaviour in an in-patient context. The idea is to motivate anorexics by positively reinforcing their efforts to gain weight along with their actual weight increases. With bulimics the aim is positively to reinforce the absence of bulimic symptoms. Other interventions used with bulimics have been exposure to binge foods and response prevention of vomiting.

Cognitive therapy (CT): This approach focuses on the anorexic's beliefs as well as behaviour. The aim is to alter the anorexic's beliefs, e.g. through retribution – helping anorexics to change their self-perceptions (e.g. perceiving themselves as fat). With regard to bulimics, distorted cognitions relating to food and body image are identified and challenged.

Substance abuse and dependence

The concepts

The two concepts of substance dependence and substance abuse are differentiated in the following ways.

Substance abuse

This is the stage before total substance dependence. Any one of the following counts as having substance abuse:

- drug-connected difficulties in going to school or keeping a job;
- using drugs in dangerous circumstances;
- drug-connected legal problems;
- persistent use of drugs despite social and personal problems.

Substance dependence

Any three out of the seven criteria below count as experiencing substance dependence:

- preoccupation with the drug;
- over-using the drug;
- developing tolerance for the drug;
- experiencing psychological and physical withdrawal symptoms;
- making continual efforts to control the use of the drug along with repeated relapses;
- neglecting social, job and leisure activities in order to use the drug;
- persisting in drug use despite serious health problems.

A significant proportion of adolescents have tried alcoholic and non-alcoholic substances. Some try drug cocktails or are polydrug users. The essential aim of most drug use is to attain a sense of elation. Habitual drug use can lead to a deterioration in physical and mental health including suicide, impaired cognitive functioning, criminality, educational and academic failure, financial problems and difficulties in maintaining close personal and family relationships. Drug abuse can be associated with other disorders such as conduct, ADHD, mood and eating disorders. Children of drug abusers may suffer from drug-related problems. With street drugs there is always a danger of impurities or accidental overdosing.

Alcohol abuse and dependence

Excessive consumption of alcohol is connected to a significant proportion of murders, suicides, juvenile delinquencies, school drop-outs, car accidents and health problems as well as the reduction of life expectancy.

Excessive alcohol use among adolescents is related to family conflicts, inadequate parenting (poor supervision, low expectations and few rewards) and heavy parental drinking. It is also connected to an adolescent's peer group abuse of alcohol, particularly if they are older adolescents. Adolescents who are easily bored and who want immediate gratification are particularly at risk.

Effects of over-use of alcohol

- acts as a brain depressant – depending on the level of alcohol it can affect motor and emotional control areas of the brain and eventually lead to respiratory and heart disturbances resulting in stupor, coma and finally death;

- can adversely disturb sleep;
- is connected to the development of health problems, e.g. cirrhosis of the liver, heart disease, various cancers and gastrointestinal problems.

Alcohol abuse and dependence are characterised as follows:

- need for regular, daily and large intakes of alcohol;
- periods of being sober interrupted by binge drinking;
- inability to cut down or stop drinking;
- experiencing blackouts when drunk;
- persistent drinking despite having health problems made worse by alcohol;
- social, occupational, legal and family problems, e.g. absence from college, work, arrests for drunkenness, traffic accidents and being verbally and physically aggressive towards family members.

Amphetamine use

Amphetamines are addictive drugs which can have the following effects on people. There are also manufactured drugs which are modified versions or analogues of drugs like amphetamines which are called 'designer drugs'. Ecstasy or MDMA is a well-known 'designer drug'.

Intoxication
- behavioural or psychological changes, e.g. euphoria, emotional blunting, anxiety, anger and tension, impaired judgement, adverse social and occupational functioning;
- physical symptoms, e.g. racing or slow heart rate, widened pupils, high or low blood pressure, perspiration or chills, nausea or vomiting and agitation or retardation.

Withdrawal effects
- dysphoria;
- physical symptoms, e.g. fatigue, vivid unpleasant dreams, insomnia or excessive sleep, agitation or retardation.

The most adverse physical effects are on the heart, e.g. heart attacks and high blood pressure, and the nervous system, e.g. seizures, coma and death.

The most adverse psychological effects are restlessness, irritability, insomnia, hostility and confusion. Anxiety and panic disorders, hallucinations and paranoid delusions can result from amphetamine use.

Designer drugs
There is increasing demand for designer drugs, e.g. ecstasy (3,4 methylene-dioxynmethylamphetamine or MDMA) in other public places besides clubs and

the price is falling. The heaviest use is among young people from 18 to 25. The drug affects the neurotransmitters serotonin and dopamine.

Use of designer drugs can bring about mood changes particularly in relating to others as people feel closer to each other and feel they can more easily communicate with one another. It can also produce feelings of euphoria, empathy, self-confidence and self-acceptance. Some users have also reported perceptual effects, e.g. after-images, geometrical patterns in the visual field and distortions of objects. Other possible effects are sweating, nausea, headaches, unsteadiness, widened pupils, rapid heart rate, insomnia, tension in the jaw, teeth clenching and grinding. After use it can also result in anxiety and depression. Bad experiences are normally the result of high doses, e.g. visual and auditory hallucinations, panic, insomnia, flashbacks and even psychosis in susceptible people. Fatalities occur due to heatstroke, water toxicity due to excessive water retention and heart failure.

Cannabis

Cannabis is a psychoactive drug containing cannabinoids which can produce the following effects:

- euphoria;
- most common physical effects: red eyes, increased appetite, dry mouth and a mildly racing heart rate.

Intoxication

- maladaptive behavioural or psychological changes, e.g. impaired co-ordination, anxiety, feeling time has slowed down, impaired judgement and withdrawal;
- physical effects, e.g. red eyes, increased appetite, dry mouth and a racing heart rate. High levels of tetrahydrocannabiniol (THC), the psychoactive part of cannabis, can precipitate paranoia and hallucinations leading eventually to a cannabis-induced schizophrenia. People prone to psychotic symptoms include those who smoke in their early teens and those who have a genetic predisposition to mental illness.

There is tolerance to the effects of the drug but there is no clear evidence of physical dependence and no psychological dependence.

Heroin

Heroin is an opiate derived from morphine. It originates from the sap of the opium poppy – *Paparver somniferum*. The raw opium has to be converted into morphine. Various chemicals and refining processes are used to produce heroin. The degree of purity depends on the manufacturing process, levels above 90 per cent are possible. The main poppy fields are located in Afghanistan, Pakistan and Myanmar (Burma) but there are also large growing areas in Columbia.

Most heroin users are polydrug users, e.g. tranquillizers, amphetamines and cocaine. Heroin can be injected (most popular method), snorted, smoked or taken as pills. Injecting heroin can lead to HIV, and hepatitis B and C.

Heroin imitates the effect of endorphins which kill pain through decreasing nerve impulses that communicate pain. It can have a serious effect on breathing, cause flushing, sweating and itching and also cause vomiting and constipation. Conspicuous effects include the constriction of the pupils to pinpoints along with slurred speech and a slow gait.

The sought-after effect is euphoria and the removal of tension and anxiety.

Heroin abusers may neglect their appearance and fail to eat and sleep sufficiently creating health problems. Excessive spending on the drug may also lead to poor living conditions. Long-term heath problems include skin and pulmonary abscesses, septicaemia, collapsing veins, infections of blood vessels and heart, liver and respiratory disease. Overdosing is a serious risk due to drug impurities and adulteration of the drug. Overdosing may lead to coma and death. Mental health problems include depression and mood swings. Women may be at risk of irregular periods and, if pregnant, of miscarriage, of low weight babies and premature birth.

Heroin produces a high degree of tolerance and physical dependence. Withdrawal conditions occur if the drug is stopped or reduced. These conditions include aches, spasms, diarrhoea, goose bumps, tremors, chills and kicking movements. Psychological dependence takes the form of feeling unable to cope with life without the drug.

Cocaine and crack use

Cocaine is a drug derived from the coca plant, a member of the genus *Erythroxyum*, and tends to be used by older adolescents. The main growing areas are in South America, particularly in Columbia, Bolivia and Peru.

Cocaine is an alkaloid, very addictive and can be highly dangerous, e.g. heart attacks. Injecting cocaine can lead to hepatitis C. It works by concentrating the neurotransmitter dopamine in the synapses between neurones. This high can last 40 to 60 minutes after which another intake is necessary to maintain the high.

Crack is a very powerful form of cocaine and is highly addictive. Crack addicts need large sums of cash to feed the habit and this can induce them to resort to street robberies. Crack is used by some along with heroin. Addicts can become suspicious, secretive and aggressive.

Effects of cocaine
- It has an effect almost immediately and lasts briefly (30 to 60 minutes).
- Psychological dependence can occur.
- Tolerance and sensitivity to its effects can occur after repeated use.

- Physical dependence does happen but withdrawal is relatively mild compared to that of opiates.

Intoxication

- psychological effects: elation, euphoria, raised self-esteem, perceived improvement in performance. High intake can lead to agitation, irritability, impaired judgement and aggression. Paranoid delusions and auditory hallucinations can also occur.
- physical effects: increased blood pressure and heart rate, headaches, nausea, nasal problems, damage to lungs, breathing difficulties, intravenous use carries possibility of HIV infection/hepatitis C, heart problems (irregular heartbeat, heart valve disease), stroke, seizures and death.

Withdrawal effects

- dysphoria, anxiety, irritability, fatigue and being awake a great deal;
- craving for the drug can be extremely powerful.

Hallucinogen use

Hallucinogenic drugs are sometimes called psychedelics or psychomimetics. They produce hallucinations but also they lead to loss of contact with reality and feelings of an expanded consciousness.

LSD (lysergic acid diethylamide) is one of the main forms of hallucinogenic drug. There is no physical dependence and no withdrawal symptoms but a psychological dependence can develop related to feelings of having an expanded consciousness. Tolerance occurs and reverses quickly. Effects include tremors, high heart rate, high blood pressure, sweating, blurring of vision and death can occur. Intense and brilliant colours are seen and other senses are also heightened. There are also changes in body image and one's perception of space and time. Visual hallucinations occur. Feelings become more intense. There are feelings of religious, mystical and philosophical insight.

Intoxication

- psychological changes: anxiety, depression, ideas of reference, fear of going mad, paranoia, impaired social and job performance and a bad trip;
- perceptual changes: heightened perception, feelings of unreality, feelings of losing one's sense of self, illusions, hallucinations and flashbacks;
- physical symptoms: widened pupils, rapid heartbeat, sweating, palpitations, blurring of sight, tremors and lack of co-ordination.

Inhalant use

There is a relatively high use of inhalants, e.g. solvents, glues, aerosols, paint thinners and lighter fuels among adolescents and high use is also connected with an increased probability of juvenile delinquency. Inhalants are depressants and rapidly affect the brain. Tolerance can develop. In small amounts the effects can be euphoria, excitement and pleasant feelings.

Intoxication

Can lead to apathy, nausea, dizziness, lack of co-ordination, slurred speech, unsteadiness, tremor, impaired social and job functioning and impulsive or aggressive behaviour. High intake levels can also result in anxiety, illusions, auditory and visual hallucinations, distortions of body image, stupor and unconsciousness.

Withdrawal effects

Withdrawal effects are not common but when they do occur they can take the form of sleep problems, irritability, sweating, nausea, vomiting, rapid heart rate and on occasion delusions and hallucinations.

Smoking

Many smokers start the addiction in early adolescence and smoking is on the increase among adolescents. Adolescent smokers are more likely to be involved in delinquent activities than non-smokers.

Effects

Users report that smoking improves attention, learning and problem-solving and also reduces anxious and depressive feelings. Premature death can eventually result, e.g. through emphysema, lung cancer and heart problems.

Withdrawal effects

Can be nausea, vomiting, stomach pain, diarrhoea, dizziness, tremor, headache, raised blood pressure and heart rate.

Adolescent substance use and abuse

Many adolescents experiment with drugs but do not go on to problematic use. Furthermore, many adolescents tend to move in and out of drug use and move away from it completely without any formal intervention.

Drugs are used for a variety of reasons, e.g. pleasure, curiosity, excitement, reducing or relieving tension and boredom, to achieve status in the eyes of one's peers, to be part of the rave or dance culture, as a means of enhancing performance and as a way of coping with problems.

Substance abuse can adversely affect school and college achievement, produce health problems, lead to road accidents and impair social and personal relationships. Furthermore, drug abuse is associated with conduct disorders, delinquency and unemployment.

There are a variety of **risk factors** for substance abuse; there is no one single set of factors. These factors are as follows: age of first use, early initiation, early behavioural problems at school, school failure, low self-esteem, unconventional lifestyle, parental and sibling use, negative relationships with parents, inadequate parenting (inconsistency and poor supervision), peer pressure and imitation, sensation-seeking, impulsivity, availability and cost, and neighbourhood decay.

Social learning theory sees adolescent substance abuse as resulting from modelling and reinforcement. Individuals imitate parental or peer drug use and receive reinforcement from the pleasurable effects of the drug.

Problem behaviour theory sees substance abuse as one problem amidst a group or syndrome of adolescent problem behaviours and unconventional beliefs that amount to a deviant lifestyle. Drug use may enable an adolescent to join a particular peer group, or be a means of coping with, for example, school failure, anxiety or rejection.

Social stress theory sees substance abuse as related to adolescent stress levels.

Family systems theory sees substance abuse as resulting from negative family influences and interactions. Parental rejection, parent drug use, parental permissive attitudes towards drugs, punitive and authoritarian parenting and older siblings' drug use all contribute towards adolescent substance abuse.

Treatment of adolescent substance abuse has been through family therapy, community-based programmes and cognitive-behavioural approaches. However, treatment is difficult because motivation is either weak or absent, hence preventative approaches have assumed a higher priority. Preventative approaches include educational programmes which involve teachers and peers and are community-linked and programmes designed to develop social skills that enable adolescents to resist peer pressure and enhance self-esteem.

Assessment

Assessment is undertaken through physical examination including urine analysis, structured interviews and psychological questionnaires.

Risk factors include behavioural and emotional problems, learning difficulties, academic problems, positive attitudes and values towards drug use and a proclivity for risk-taking. Other factors include attachment problems and inadequate parenting, parental drug abuse and parental criminality. Social factors influencing drug abuse include drug availability, peer pressure, bullying, change of school, loss of friendships and involvement in a deviant peer group. Drug abuse may be maintained through the desire to avoid negative moods, relationship problems and educational difficulties. Other factors maintaining drug abuse include low self-efficacy, denial of the problem, drug-abusing parents and inadequate parental supervision, inconsistent parental discipline, chaotic family communication and a deprived neighbourhood where there are few alternatives or opportunities. There is a tendency for substance abuse to occur along with mental disorders such as anxiety and depression and also with anti-social behaviour, delinquency, teenage pregnancy, school behavioural difficulties, truancy, self-harm, suicide and accident fatalities and injuries. Early onset of drug use is a negative sign and regular and high consumption of drugs and alcohol is associated with problems in adult life.

Formulation

A formulation will integrate information from physical examination, interviews and psychological questionnaires. It should be determined whether there is a transient or experimental use of drugs or alternatively habitual use of drugs. It is necessary also to ascertain the degree of determination and commitment to change the current situation.

Interventions

General points include the need to determine the level of motivation for change, to educate the drug abuser, the family and other care providers on the particular drug and the concomitant signs and risks of abuse. There may be an underlying psychiatric disorder, parental and family conflict and academic failure at school or college. Where there are medical complications, medical treatment may be required. Detoxification is a phase in the treatment process during which the physical effects of withdrawal are dealt with. The focus should be on all of the adolescent's current problems as well as on substance abuse and also on the adolescent's fears and expectations. Persuasion not force should be used to stop adolescents taking drugs and any improvements such as drug reduction should be reinforced. It will also be necessary to treat any anxiety or depression that the adolescent is experiencing. Self-help groups, e.g. Nar-Anon along with parent support groups are useful, particularly in the follow-up period.

Biological approaches focus on the disorders that may occur along with substance abuse such as anxiety and depression.

Multi-systemic approaches include family therapy and individually and community-based interventions. The focus is on changing inappropriate family interactions that maintain adolescent substance abuse. The aims of family therapy include developing parental partnerships that help change adolescent drug abuse, goal and rule setting, developing alternatives to substance use after the substance-taking has ceased and accessing self-help groups. Individually based interventions include behavioural and cognitive-behavioural approaches, social and problem-solving skills training and assertiveness training. These approaches may be combined with family therapy. Community-based interventions include school counselling and self-help groups.

Juvenile delinquency

The concept

Juvenile delinquency is defined as the committing of legal offences by young people; criminal responsibility is set at 10 years of age and the upper limit for juvenile delinquency is set at 17 years of age.

Delinquents

Delinquency starts in early adolescence, around 11 to 12 years, and then reaches a peak in middle and late teens. More males than females are delinquents; there is also an association with low social status and controversy over the rates of delinquency among ethnic minorities.

Delinquents are more likely than non-delinquents to have been involved in truancy, vandalism, fighting, disobedience, lying, theft and bullying. There is also likely to be a lack of attachment to parents. They often come from stressed families where parents are in conflict and where parents manifest criminal behaviour. In these families parental supervision, monitoring, communication and affection towards the adolescent are also inadequate or inconsistent. There is also an association between delinquency and large family size. Attentional and hyperactivity problems are also apparent and there are low levels of academic achievement among delinquents. Delinquents are frequently unpopular with their peers but are not socially isolated. They also tend to be heavy drinkers, smokers and gamblers and sexually active at a younger age.

Theories of delinquency

There are sociological, psychological and biological theories as to why delinquency occurs.

Sociological theories emphasise the influence of social factors on the origins of delinquency:

- **Anomie/strain theory (Merton, 1938)**: delinquency arises from the gap between an adolescent's material goals and the means of achieving those goals, e.g. due to educational failure.
- **Sub-cultural theory (Mays, 1972)**: delinquency is seen as the 'norm' for a specific subcultural group and is learned by an adolescent through association with that subcultural group.
- **Differential association theory (Sutherland, 1939)**: delinquency is learned by an adolescent through association with delinquents and others engaging in criminal behaviour.
- **Labelling theory (Lemert, 1972)**: when an adolescent is labelled as a delinquent then that adolescent is more likely to engage in delinquency in the future.

Psychological theories emphasise the influence of psychological factors on delinquency:

- **Psychoanalytic theories** emphasise that children have unconscious biological aggressive and destructive drives which need to be controlled through internalising moral controls from their parents. Delinquency is seen as the acting out of unresolved unconscious conflicts.
- Learning theories state that delinquent behaviour is learned like any other behaviour, i.e. it is acquired, performed and maintained through learning, mainly operant conditioning processes.

Delinquent behaviour occurs because parents fail to provide appropriate conditions for adolescents to avoid delinquency; instead they create conditions that encourage delinquency, e.g. lack of rules, lack of monitoring, lack of labelling specific acts as right or wrong, inconsistency in dealing with appropriate and inappropriate behaviour, a lack of warmth and excessive reliance on punishment.

Biological theories emphasise the influence of genetically influenced personality factors as contributing to delinquent behaviour.

Interventions

- **Behavioural**: these approaches start with the operant premises that delinquent behaviour is reinforced by its consequences.
- **Token economies**: in an institutional setting 'token economies', i.e. earning privileges through a system of tokens, have been set up positively to reinforce desired behaviour but those behaviours may not generalise beyond that particular institution.
- **Parent-training programmes**: parents are encouraged to use positive reinforcement with their children, to avoid punishment, to monitor their children's social activities, to be decisive in dealing with deviant behaviour, to negotiate behaviour contracts and to acquire problem-solving skills.
- **Counselling and psychotherapeutic approaches**: such approaches have not been seen as successful with most delinquents although those who are anxious, introspective, willing to discuss their personal problems and who show insight may benefit.
- **Teachers and delinquency**: schools are seen as having a role in reducing pupil behavioural problems that may lead to delinquency. Schools can help by developing whole-school behaviour policies based on the Elton Report (1989). Teachers can help to reduce behavioural problems by avoiding high levels of punishment, by positively reinforcing desirable behaviour, by modelling appropriate behaviours, by using effective classroom management strategies and by providing opportunities for pupils to act responsibly.
- **Parents and delinquency**: parents can help to reduce the likelihood of delinquency by positively reinforcing their children's appropriate behaviour, by making sure that their children know the law and rules of conduct, by adequately supervising and monitoring their children's social activities, by ensuring that they consistently show disapproval of undesirable behaviours and by taking time to discuss their children's concerns in an authoritative but non-authoritarian way.

Families and adolescence

The concept of the family

Families can be seen as social **systems** which have established a set of rules, which have ascribed and assigned roles, a power structure and strategies for solving disputes. There are different types of families, e.g. nuclear, extended, step- and single parent. These families have **subsystems** which are the spouse, parent and sibling subsystems. These subsystems can mutually influence one another.

- **Adolescents and step-families**: where reorganisation of a family occurs through a step-father appearing, he may be seen as an unwanted interloper and his authority rejected by his partner's children; this in turn can adversely affect the couple's relationship. If the step-father brings his own children into the family, this may create conflict between his children and the other children.

- **Adolescent mothers**: these mothers may experience a number of problems such as the absence of supportive fathers, low levels of educational achievement, unemployment, low income levels and child-rearing difficulties.

- **Homosexual parents and adolescents**: this is a family where homosexual parents bring up adolescent children either as a couple or as a single parent. Some children may be the result of previous heterosexual relationships, others may be the result of AIDs or some equivalent process. Such parents may confront hostility from other adults along the lines that such parenting is 'unnatural', that a child needs both a male and female parent, that a boy needs a male role model, that the child will grow up as a homosexual or will be molested. Adolescent sons and daughters may experience hostility from other children and also have their own reservations about their parents' sexual orientation.

- **Multicultural parents and adolescents**: this is a family where parents come from different ethnic groups and who have children that are of mixed ethnicity. Adolescents may experience conflicts over their ethnic and cultural identities.

Parental styles and adolescence: various categories have been proposed, e.g.:

The two continuums of:

- **permissiveness/restrictiveness**: allowing their children excessive freedom and having few consistently applied rules or hardly allowing them any freedom;

- **warmth/hostility**: showing affection and approval, giving praise and enjoying the company of their children, or displaying coldness, disapproval or indifference towards them. The above characteristics can appear in various combinations.

Patterns of parental styles:

- **authoritarian**: parents depending on coercion alone to control their children rather than reasoning with them or praising them;

- **permissive**: parents who do not consistently enforce rules and who do not have high expectations of their children;

- **authoritative**: parents who maintain firm control over their children through reasoning with their children rather than depending on coercion;

- **rejecting/neglecting**: parents who do not provide supervision, who do not have any expectations and who are not supportive of their children.

There are debates and controversies over different types of families, e.g. patriarchal, heterosexual, homosexual, and single-parent families.

Family difficulties and adolescence

Problems may arise within families due to scapegoating an individual member – they become a symptom-bearer for the whole family, the differing perspectives of family members, the point reached in the family life cycle – difficulties may arise in negotiating transitions and responsibilities, the desire for independence, triangular relationships between family members, marital and family conflict.

A person with an emotional or behavioural difficulty disturbs the equilibrium of the family and exacerbates problems within other family members. The family may scapegoat a member. This process may in turn result in the creation of factional conflicts.

Common issues that arise between parents and adolescents

The following issues can often arise between parents and their adolescent children: staying out late, wearing particular types of clothes or adornments, untidy rooms, choice of friends, sexual relationships, drinking alcohol and taking drugs.

It is useful for parents to consider the following points:

- in their youth they may have engaged in and survived the very things that they condemn in their adolescent children; that other parents find these issues arising with their own children;
- that adolescents may feel the need to rebel and oppose their parents in order to form their own personal identity and to develop a sense of autonomy in preparation for adulthood;
- that adolescents may on the surface resent and reject parental advice and guidance but really appreciate parents who care and who provide a secure base;
- that adolescents would rather have parents who set boundaries than have parents who do not set limits at all;
- that there should be a balance between tight and lax supervision – tight control as well as laxity can evoke and maintain adolescent deviance;
- that parents should consider trying some of the approaches and strategies outlined previously;
- that adolescents generally appreciate listening parents who consider and discuss their views even if the parents think those views are misguided;
- that adolescent children who go through a period of instability nevertheless can survive and flourish as adults;
- that adolescents may find it difficult to cope with the arrival of a step-father or step-mother with their own children.

Family assessment

Methods of obtaining information include structured interviews, self-report questionnaires and observation. Genograms, or family trees, are often used to summarise relationships and issues within the family. Multi-method assessment is used to present an overall view of families. Family assessment includes the following aspects: physical health problems, and emotional and behavioural difficulties of the adolescent. With regard to the parents it is necessary to know their physical and psychological health and about any parental conflict, parental control, parenting history, parent–adolescent interactions, parenting style and care. Other aspects include how far there is closeness and distance within the family, the existence of power hierarchies and the emotional climate.

Case studies

Depressed 18-year-old student

Self-referral

Sarah is a bright 18-year-old 'A' level student who feels that her mood swings interfere with her aim of securing university entrance. She has gained her teachers' respect and expects high grades in her final exams. However, because Sarah did not do well in her mocks she wants to explore ways of coping with her moods.

Presenting problems

Sarah sees herself as attractive in appearance but wants people to accept her for her personality, not her looks. Even her friends appear to prefer others to her. She does not like to be on her own, even for an evening. She misses course deadlines, as well as lessons. Sarah says that even though she believes her parents love her, they do not have time to be with her.

A psychodynamic approach to understanding Sarah's background

Sarah's parents divorced before she was one year old. She has always lived with her busy mother who treats her like a friend. Sarah admires her mother's independent lifestyle but feels isolated from her at times, particularly missing her support when faced with crises, e.g. examination anxiety or a break-up with her boyfriend.

Her father has remarried and has two more children, an 11-year-old half-sister and a 14-year-old half-brother. He is now in the process of a second divorce. Sarah was perplexed by this and said that it revived memories of feelings of loss and separation, which she found difficult to talk about. She finds it easier to talk about her brother's or sister's feelings than her own.

By distancing her anxiety over her own feelings (e.g. her jealousy of her siblings, her rivalry towards her mother for her father's affection and her anger over her father's absence), she is able to maintain some control over those feelings.

Sarah appears to seek approval from everyone she meets and feels unhappy if they do not admire her. Her last boyfriend had been unfaithful to her and Sarah felt betrayed and in despair and finished the relationship.

Sarah relates to others in the same way that she relates to her parents. She wants approval and thinks that unless it is forthcoming she has been rejected. Sarah feels, if only she was vivacious, people would seek out her company.

Sarah's perspective

Sarah believes her mood swings affect the way she copes with her life. She blames herself for not being self-disciplined and that, if she were, then she would succeed at her studies and gain everyone's love and admiration. She feels her whole family expects her to be successful and that she cannot live up to these expectations. Sarah needs to attain high grades at 'A' level to prove herself in everyone's eyes.

She has problems in sleeping, with racing thoughts about the day's events, particularly worrying about what she had said to whom. She has experimented with drugs and sex because she wants to gain peer acceptance. But she then feels guilty, worthless and hopeless, seeing herself as letting her parents down. As a result, she loses pleasure in everything and absents herself from college to avoid facing others who appear superior in her eyes.

Counsellor's assessment

Sarah displays many signs of depressive feelings:

- sleep problems;

- feelings of guilt, worthlessness, hopelessness and helplessness;

- makes negative social comparisons with others;

- experiments with drugs and sex as a way of coping with her problems;

- experiences a loss of interest and pleasure in life;

- worries excessively over what she has said to others;

- fears social isolation.

Counsellor's psychodynamic formulation

Sarah is finding it difficult to cope with her moods. She is experiencing depressive feelings over her lack of academic achievement and over her family and personal relationships. She fears that she will become socially isolated and forgotten.

Unconsciously, Sarah's actions are an attempt to gain her parents' attention and affection, particularly her father's. She gained some temporary relief through taking drugs and having sex but depressive feelings returned as she started to feel guilty over her behaviour. Sarah then plunged into a cycle of hopelessness and despair.

Counselling interventions

The counsellor chose an eclectic approach to Sarah's problems:

Psychodynamic	The aim was to work with the transference and counter-transference between Sarah and the counsellor, particularly with respect to Sarah's feelings towards her parents and the underlying feelings of loss and separation.
Person-centred	The aim of the counsellor was to display empathy, unconditional regard and congruence towards Sarah, such that she could feel that her problems were understood in a non-judgemental way. Another aim was to enable Sarah to

	draw upon her own internal resources to cope with problems.
Cognitive	The aim was to identify and challenge Sarah's negative cognitive processes, e.g. her belief that she must be admired by everyone and that if this is not forthcoming, she is being rejected. The aim was also to outline the connection between her beliefs, her depressive feelings and the consequences of those feelings.

Counselling evaluation

The aim is to evaluate progress towards the alleviation of Sarah's depressive feelings based upon:

- the gradual return of feelings of hope and self-worth;

- resolving or coming to terms with underlying feelings of loss and separation;

- increasing attendance at college;

- greater effort put into her studies;

- avoidance of drugs and sex as a means of coping with her problems;

- changing the belief that she must be liked by everyone.

CASE STUDY

Managing a sexual relationship

Introduction
Joy is a 17-year-old female student, studying for a vocational course. She is confused about how to manage her many relationships and specifically her sexual relationship with her boyfriend. She recognises that her non-assertive personality interferes with her need to succeed in developing appropriate relationships and to progress satisfactorily in her studies.

Presenting problem
Joy finds that she is upset and sad a lot of the time. She is usually tearful and quiet, saying that it is difficult to express verbally how she feels. She sees her relationship with her boyfriend as the main cause of her distress. She wants to be able to see him regularly, have other friends, spend time with her family and achieve in her studies, but feels that she cannot manage all the demands on her.

Family background
Joy is the youngest member of her family, living with both her parents and two older sisters. Both sets of grandparents live nearby and Joy spends a lot of her time visiting them. She feels that her parents have brought her up in the Roman Catholic faith and she used to be very religious when young. Her older sister left school as soon as she could and is working in a job with prospects. Her middle sister is a high achiever and is studying hard, determined to be successful academically. Joy does not feel intelligent or capable.

Adolescent's perspective
Joy feels that she cannot achieve in her studies because she is not clever and she is also upset about her relationship with her boyfriend. She feels that she is not studying very hard because she is not intelligent, otherwise she thinks she ought to be able to concentrate. She feels her boyfriend dominates her, is jealous of her and won't allow her any independence. She wants to be able to relate to friends and family without feeling guilty that she is letting him down.

She feels drawn into a sexual relationship with her boyfriend which makes her feel guilty and unsafe. Although she takes the contraceptive pill, she feels that he is not taking responsibility for safe sex and the responsibility makes her feel burdened. She wants to be a 'good girl' and feels that sex before marriage is sinful. She says that she does not enjoy sex but pretends to do so to please her boyfriend. She thinks that she is developing a phobia about being alone with her boyfriend as he will want sex and she will try to find some excuse to avoid the sexual act.

She is seeking counselling in order to help herself develop assertiveness and independence and the ability to concentrate on her studies.

A psychodynamic approach to understanding the adolescent's problems
Joy is ambivalent and confused about her identity and her relationships to others. She wants to study effectively and communicate well, and spend more time with her family. Her inability to concentrate indicates that she is trying to avoid thinking about her confused feelings so she avoids studying as it stimulates her thinking. She then imagines she is not intelligent and feels that she cannot relate well to others because her boyfriend is demanding a lot of her

attention. She feels she is in love with her boyfriend and wants to see him often but feels drawn into a sexual relationship which makes her feel guilty.

Joy feels she wants to be a 'good girl' to be accepted by her family but her guilt because of her sexual relationship is reinforcing her feelings of isolation and separation. She seems to be drawn into a sexual relationship with her boyfriend so that she can feel accepted and wanted. Her jealousy of her siblings who seem to be achieving in their different spheres is exacerbating her feelings of inadequacy, and reinforcing her feelings of low self-esteem.

She relates to others as if she were younger than her years, seeking approval through her passivity and acquiescence. She wants to please so that she can be accepted and she fears that sex or competitive feelings will be considered unacceptable and she will be rejected.

She is in danger of developing sexual problems as she cannot allow herself to enjoy a sexual relationship, yet at the same time she is participating in sexual activities against her will. It can be considered that she can only have sex under the pretence that she is pleasing her boyfriend, thus avoiding taking responsibility for her actions. This ambivalence reflects her approach to life – being unable to make up her mind about what suits her. Through counselling she hopes to find out her preferences and her identity.

Counsellor's assessment
Joy displays many signs of an adolescent who is becoming depressed and anxious because of her desire to be accepted and behave in a moral way:

● confused and ambivalent about her identity;

● does not allow herself to think about her confused and overwhelming feelings;

● talks negatively of the sexual act;

● does not enjoy sexual experimentation;

● feels she is having sex to please someone else;

● feelings of jealousy and competitiveness;

● tries to please others through being passive.

Counsellor's psychodynamic formulation
Joy is finding it difficult coping with her passivity in relation to others. She fears that she tries to please by giving what she thinks others want. She acquiesces to sex with her boyfriend and then feels guilty, thus reinforcing the feeling that she is passive and immoral. She wants to be able to be independent, yet fears isolation and rejection.

Unconsciously Joy's passivity and lack of assertiveness are her way of not taking responsibility for her actions. Her secondary gain of being passive is that others tell her what to do so that she does not have to think for herself. Her defence mechanism is her denial of her capabilities and her intelligence. The denial of her attributes results in her being able to study effectively, and because she does not allow herself to think, she continues to remain passive.

Joy's unconscious denial of her innermost feelings is her difficulty in acknowledging that her feelings, projections and the way she handles her relationships have a direct correlation in what happens in her life and how people treat her.

Counsellor's interventions

Psychodynamic

The aim is to work with the transference and counter-transference to help Joy understand that her learned past behaviour and the way she behaves now are linked.

Working with the transference will help Joy recognise that she relates to others, in this case her counsellor, as if the counsellor is authoritarian and rejecting like she imagines her parents were when she was a child. This will enable her to recognise that she imagines that everyone can be authoritarian and rejecting and she herself has to remain a passive obedient child so as not to evoke these feeling in others.

In this case, the counter-transference feeling evoked in the counsellor was a desire to tell Joy what to do about her relationship with her boyfriend. This awareness will enable the counsellor to make sense of Joy's inner world and understand Joy's behaviour. This understanding will be useful in that the counsellor is now able to understand the dynamic between Joy and her boyfriend. Joy cannot finish her relationship with her boyfriend because she expects him to behave in an authoritarian and demanding way, and she cannot be more assertive with him as her passivity evokes his domineering behaviour.

Person-centred

The aim is to help Joy, through the counsellor's empathy, acceptance and congruence, believe that she does not have to be a 'good girl' all the time for others to like her.

In this case, the counsellor's empathy and acceptance helped the adolescent realise and recognise that she can be liked even though she has feelings which she thought unacceptable, such as anger and jealousy. In recognising that she does not have to be perfect, Joy's self-esteem can increase so that she will not feel the need to please everyone all the time.

Cognitive

The aim is to identify and challenge Joy's negative cognitive processes, e.g. her belief that she is not capable or clever, which leads her to behave passively and not study hard. The aim is to help her understand, acknowledge and challenge her beliefs which lead her to accept her passivity and lack of independence. One of the ways of doing this is to point out her successes so far and help her congratulate herself on her achievements. She can, at the end of every day, find something positive she has achieved that day and point it out to herself. She can practise expressing what she wants by asking her friends, sisters, boyfriend or parents to provide something they would gladly give. As her confidence increases, her requests can become more complex and her manner more assertive.

Counselling evaluation

The aim is to evaluate progress towards the alleviation of Joy's passivity, fear of sex and lack of studying by doing the following:

- encouraging the gradual return of feelings of self-worth;

- resolving and coming to terms with the underlying feelings of jealousy of her sisters;

- increasing her study output;

- developing her ability to express what she might want;

- developing her ability to refuse her boyfriend's requests if and when she does not want to comply with his wishes;

- changing the belief that she must please everyone.

Substance abuse

Self-referral

Tony is a 19-year-old 'A' level student who is under-achieving in his studies. His concentration and memory are poor probably because of the abuse of drugs over at least six years. He is undernourished, and suffers from sleep deprivation and hallucinations. His fear of going mad paralyses his attempts to think about his problems and he denies many of his feelings.

Presenting problem

Tony is worried that he has damaged his ability to think because he has experimented with many types of drugs over a long period of time. He wants to be like his peer group whom he thinks are able to drink, smoke, take drugs, stay up all night and still perform well in their studies. He feels that if only he could find a way to control his unbearable fear of going mad, then he will succeed in his aim to be like normal adolescents who can defy the rules and not suffer the consequences of their behaviour. He is looking for reassurance that his symptoms will go away and that he can succeed in getting to university.

Family background

Tony's parents divorced when he was only 5 years old but he remembers this as the most horrific experience of his life. He adores his father whom he sees often and is determined to emulate. His mother is busy bringing up children by her second marriage and seems to see Tony as mature enough to take responsibility for his own welfare. Tony hates his quiet and withdrawn step-father and avoids him whenever possible. He seems to like his two much younger step-siblings and sees their future as much brighter than his because they have a stable family home.

The adolescent's perspective

Tony feels that his problems started when he was 14 when he began noticing that after taking drugs or after drinking he felt weak, tired, unable to concentrate and could not think clearly. His symptoms got worse as he grew older and he noticed that he did not put on weight and could not sleep at night. He compares himself with his peers whom he sees as rebellious and over-indulgent yet good at their studies and also able to develop strong muscular bodies. He sees his father as a person who has abused his body but is still able to enjoy his life and continue to drink heavily without any seemingly adverse effects. He feels isolated, lonely and different and is frightened that he is going mad because he cannot control his fears. He feels that he has damaged his brain cells because of substance abuse and wants reassurance that if he gave up drugs, drink and cigarettes then his symptoms would disappear. He believes that no one is concerned about his welfare as everyone, especially his mother, is too busy to notice his behaviour; yet he admits that he is good at hiding the truth from people who have a reason to ask him questions, even his own GP.

A psychodynamic way of looking at the adolescent's problems

Tony is addicted to drugs, alcohol and cigarettes as a way of escaping from his uncomfortable feelings. He wants to identify with his father and peers and does not want to see himself as different from them. He fears that his feelings of isolation and loneliness mean that he is not normal. He is desperate to be noticed and is looking to bond with another who might relieve him of his anxieties in a magical way through reassurance that everything will be all right in the long run.

His anxiety about the damage he has caused himself through the substance abuse is one way of unconsciously keeping his feelings under control. He is jealous of his siblings and peers; he is envious of his father; he hates his step-father; he is angry with his mother; he is terrified of madness.

Studying stimulates his thoughts and he cannot employ his defence of distancing his overwhelming feelings of anger and jealousy, or his desire to identify with his father. He, therefore, unconsciously avoids concentrating on studying and takes refuge in his addictions. His addictive behaviour makes him feel guilty, out of control, isolated and the whole cycle begins again as he has to resort to his escape route to forget about his uncomfortable feelings.

Counsellor's assessment
Tony displays many signs of a person suffering from addictive behaviour:

- abusing substances, e.g. excessive drinking and smoking and drug-taking;

- no appetite for food;

- cannot sleep at nights;

- his feelings of anxiety, fear, anger, isolation, jealousy are overwhelming.

Counsellor's psychodynamic formulation
Tony is finding it difficult to cope with his overwhelming feelings. He is experiencing panic over what he feels is his inability to manage and control his life and his relationships. He compares himself unfavourably to others and his fears are paralysing his self-esteem. He resorts to substance abuse as his escape mechanism from reality.

When he studies, his thoughts are re-activated and he experiences the pain that his uncomfortable feelings stimulate in him.

Tony's narcissistic behaviour of unconsciously believing that he can be indestructible is his way of escaping from accepting his limitations and not taking responsibility for his feelings and behaviour. His primary gain of the continuation of his addiction is some temporary relief from his fears and anxieties.

Counselling interventions
The counsellor chose to work in an eclectic way with this adolescent because of the multi-faceted nature of his problems.

Referrals

- referral to the GP because of hallucinations, under-nourishment, lack of sleep;

- referral to a specialist drug unit because of the addiction to substances.

Psychodynamic
The aim is to work with the transference (e.g. where Tony is angry that the counsellor cannot find a miraculous solution to his problems and blames the counsellor for not caring, just as he blames his mother for not having enough time to look after him and protect him from his addictive behaviour), in order to help the counsellor understand how Tony's inner world functions (e.g. not separating from his mother). The counsellor, using this method, can make use of counter-transference (e.g. the counsellor's feelings of inadequacy in not

providing Tony with a cure) and can help the counsellor understand what the client feels.

The counsellor can use this knowledge to make interpretations that will help the client make meaning of his feelings, thoughts and behaviour. For the client to experience his feelings in a safe setting and know the consistency of the approach will in time help him to make choices of how he wants to behave.

Person-centred
The aim of the counsellor displaying empathy, unconditional regard and congruence towards Tony is so that he can begin to feel that he is understood in a non-judgemental way. The purpose of this approach is that the client can begin to feel that he is valued as a person in his own right despite his problems. This can help create an atmosphere where Tony can gain some ego strength to start coping with his problems.

Cognitive
The aim is to identify and challenge Tony's negative cognitive processes, e.g. his belief that he must be able to do anything because young men should be able to study, make relationships, abuse substances and have fun without having problems. The purpose is to outline the connection between his beliefs and his feelings of inadequacy and the consequences of his continuing to believe that he can do anything and, despite his fears, that he will succeed in his aims.

Counselling evaluation
The aim is to evaluate progress towards the alleviation of Tony's uncomfortable feelings which in turn will help Tony to stop his need to be addicted to substances:

- resolving or coming to terms with his uncomfortable feelings, e.g. his anger at his parents' divorce; his jealousy of his peers;

- the gradual belief in his own limitations;

- increase in his ability to study more effectively by learning to concentrate;

- a change in his belief that he must identify with others in order to be normal;

- less dependency on substance abuse as a way of coping with his problems.

CASE STUDY

Eating disorder

Sonia is an intelligent 18-year-old, first-year university student, who is having problems with eating. She is slim and slight, and has not menstruated in four months. She is a high achiever, yet finds it difficult to concentrate on her studies and achieve her potential. She misses her home especially her brother and sister. Although she has a lot of friends from her old school, she finds it difficult to get to know people in her halls of residence or in her classes. She feels depressed and unable to relax and is aware that she is constantly worrying about her weight and thinks of food constantly. She wants to explore her feelings as a first step to understanding herself and find ways to cope with her eating problems, her depression and her studies.

Presenting problems

Sonia sees herself as a person who tries very hard to achieve in all spheres of her life. Yet she feels that her problems hinder her progress. She feels stuck and unable to find ways forward despite her efforts. She feels exhausted, very sad, upset and angry a lot of the time. She believes that she can get to know people if she tried a bit harder, but worries that they would notice she does not eat and she cannot bear the thought that anyone would criticise her about her eating habits. She likes being thin; it gives her a sense of power and makes her feel more acceptable and able to fit in. She misses home and feels that her brother and sister will bond even more without her and would stop thinking of her. She believes her parents are supportive but they are too busy with their careers to worry about her.

Family background

Sonia's parents argue a lot and this makes her angry. She feels that her siblings will suffer as a result and worries that she is not there to look after them. Both parents have demanding jobs and put pressure on the children to achieve academically. Both parents are aware of food as they are often on diets to stay healthy to help them with middle age. Her brother is older and seems to be the one member of the family who understands her, but he is preoccupied with efforts to find a job as he has recently qualified. Her younger sister is cute and pretty and everyone likes her.

The adolescent's perspective

Sonia believes that her problems started when she started menstruating. She became moody and withdrawn, unable to make herself heard in such a busy family. She started trying to control her food intake as a way of drawing attention to herself but no one took any notice. She felt ambivalent about this; on the one hand, pleased that she could get on with eating what she liked and, on the other, annoyed and upset that her family did not see what she was doing.

At school people started complimenting her on her appearance saying she looked thin, just like girls in magazines. She felt proud of herself; at least people noticed her and she felt popular for the first time in her life. This peer attention reinforced her belief that being thin is attractive and she determined never to put on any weight.

She is also ambivalent about growing up, as she does not feel able to take responsibility for her life. She feels that having an older brother who can protect her from any unsavoury experiences is fantastic, and she would rather he lived nearby to look after her. Yet she wants to find her own way in the world and succeed academically to please her parents who are now getting old. She works for long hours perfecting her work and worries if what she completes is not of the best quality.

She came to seek help for her eating problems because she realises that thoughts of food are occupying a large part of her mind. Now that she is in a different environment she feels handicapped, because she is often tired, unable to join in activities, or socialise with other students.

A psychodynamic approach to understanding the adolescent's problems
Sonia is angry with her family and especially her parents for being too busy to pay her any attention. She feels left out by her family and worries that her siblings will become a couple and forget all about her. She is jealous of their closeness and wants her brother, her love object, all to herself. She cannot control how her family behaves but she can control what happens to her body.

She is ambivalent about growing up and wants to be looked after. She does not believe that she has had enough of anything. On one level she is acting out this feeling of not having enough by not eating. On the other hand she is starving herself as a way of attracting attention and care.

Peer approval reinforced her eating problems but now she worries that peers will reject her, as she cannot be similar to them. She realises that they will recognise the 'ill part of her' and she will experience their concern as criticism, which will make her feel upset, angry and left out. Again, she cannot control what others think or say but she can control her food intake.

She came to university to discover herself and although excited by the prospect of new experiences, she worries that she can never be good enough to meet the challenges. She fills her mind with 'food' as a way of filling up herself with sustenance but in so doing she empties her mind of other thoughts and feelings. She avoids thinking of the issues that concern her such as her angry feelings towards her parents; these feelings are dangerous because she cannot know in advance where they will lead her.

Counsellor's assessment
Sonia displays many signs of an eating disorder:

- Her menstrual cycle has been interrupted for over four months.

- She is under the recommended weight for her height and build.

- She associates food with fatness.

- She displays a perfectionist attitude about her studies.

- She is depressed.

- She experiences conflict in relationships.

- She displays issues of anger and control.

Counsellor's psychodynamic formulation
Sonia is finding growing up difficult; she wants independence but is frightened of growing up. She is overwhelmed by feelings of anger, abandonment, neglect, isolation and sadness. She fears that no one is able to contain the 'ill part of her' and has replaced her mother with her brother as her love object as she felt more able to control and manipulate his care of her. She does not allow herself to

think, thus the anger that she feels toward the 'monster mother' who has deserted her is unmanageable.

Her eating problems are a way of communicating. She looks at the couples around her, her parents, her siblings and she feels left out, isolated. She is crying out for care and attention and sustenance by not eating. She is like a baby in need of attention and she is making distress signals that no one is picking up. So, in order to manage her distress, she tries to control her food intake, and her body. She has had some positive reinforcement from peers in the past but she is terrified of criticism, as it will reinforce her suspicion that she is not managing to grow up well.

She wants to succeed and to please and feel comfortable but she does not know how to manage herself and her feelings, so she resorts to starvation as a way of controlling her environment.

Counsellor's interventions

The counsellor has chosen to work in an integrative way to support Sonia with her eating disorder. Sonia will be having weekly counselling sessions to address her unconscious feelings. As her weight is very low, the counsellor has decided that Sonia needs added help.

Specialist referrals were discussed.

The counsellor, with Sonia's permission and co-operation, has suggested that Sonia talk to her doctor, so that her weight and food intake can be monitored.

The doctor will also be able to refer her to a specialist **Eating Disorders Unit** or **Hospital** specialising in eating problems, if her weight plummets to dangerous levels.

Psychodynamic approach

The aim of this approach is to work with the transference and counter-transference phenomenon so that the adolescent can make meaning of her behaviour.

In this case, Sonia's transference feelings were indicated in the way she related to her counsellor. To begin with, she behaved as if the counsellor could magically give her exactly what she needed to make her well and help her relate to her family and peers in a mature way. After she realised that she needed to think, feel and talk in depth in the sessions to make progress, she became angry and despondent. However, she could not be angry with the counsellor in the same way as she could not show any negative feelings to her parents.

The counsellor was alert to her own counter-transference feelings and she paid attention to them. She was aware that her feelings towards Sonia fluctuated. Sometimes she felt real concern for this young person, and at other times she found herself irritated. Once or twice the counsellor found herself thinking of something in her own life that made her very angry. The counsellor used these feelings to inform her of Sonia's state of mind.

The counsellor was able to make transference comments after taking into consideration what Sonia said, her silences, her body language and the counter-transference feelings. One of the comments that seemed to help her was 'You don't seem to believe that I can keep you in mind between one session and the next; as if you believe that I have forgotten about you, perhaps in the same way as you believe your parents do not have time for you because they are busy with their jobs.'

Gradually, with transference comments that helped Sonia make meaning of her behaviour, the adolescent started linking the way she felt with her behaviour. She recognised that she tried through her control of food to control her environment and relieve herself from her anxieties.

Person-centred approach
The counsellor used Carl Rogers's four necessary conditions for growth: empathy, active listening, congruence and unconditional positive regard, to work with the young person. In listening and empathising, being solid and available and in accepting the adolescent as she is, the counsellor helped her to feel someone was there for her.

Gradually, Sonia was able to talk about her feelings of rejection and abandonment, anger and fear and in so doing the two participants engaged in a dialogue that helped her understand some of her behaviour.

Cognitive-behavioural
The aim of using this method is to identify and challenge Sonia's cognitive processes. She is then able to think of the connection between the way she thinks and the way she behaves, e.g. if she believes her parents are too busy to care, she behaves as if this is true and she stops caring about herself by not eating. The aim is to help her become more realistic about her behaviour, e.g. if she continued not eating, then she would become too ill to achieve her aim of succeeding and achieving at university.

Counselling evaluation
The aim is to evaluate progress towards the alleviation of Sonia's eating problems based upon:

- a change in the way the adolescent thinks and feels about herself;

- a more realistic attitude towards eating;

- weight stability;

- a more realistic outlook towards relationships;

- resolving some of her uncomfortable and unmanageable feelings.

CASE STUDY

Self-harm

Janice is a 20-year-old student who is finding it hard to study despite her obvious ability. She is tall and slim, attractive and well groomed. Despite living in a house with other students, she feels isolated. She cuts her arms and legs, and drinks rather heavily. Occasionally she bangs her head on the banisters. She worries that this is not a healthy way to live. She recognises that her work is suffering because she is not able to concentrate and fulfil her potential. She wants to stop cutting herself yet she feels she is not able to take control of her actions. She hopes that by coming to counselling she will be helped to find a way forward to stop self-harming.

Presenting problems

Janice sees herself as a person in trouble. She cannot understand her self-harming behaviour and she is concerned that she cannot stop drinking and worries that she is slowly killing herself. She feels that going to the pub or a bar is her only fun activity, but then she states that she hardly goes out, saying that everyone else she knows is paired up and she cannot go out on her own. When at university or with her housemates she feels better and more relaxed. Her predominant feeling is that she is left out and that if she could have a boyfriend then everything would be all right. She usually cuts herself in the middle of the night when others are in bed and seems to think that no one has ever noticed that she always wears long sleeves that cover her arms. She does not believe that anyone has ever seen her marked skin. She believes that she is depressed as she does not take pleasure in many things.

Family background

Janice's parents have been living together for 25 years, but she does not believe their relationship is good. Her father is an engineer who works long hours and likes leisure time in the garden. She sees her father as a strict disciplinarian who likes everything his own way. Her mother teaches in the local primary school and spends her free time experimenting with interesting food to feed her family and especially her husband whom she seems to favour. Janice thinks that her mother is a very nice, kind woman who is concerned for her and her sister but she cannot stand up to her father who seems to dominate the household. Her sister has already left home and is living in a shared flat and working full time, and is preoccupied with her own life.

The adolescent's perspective

Janice feels that she cuts when she is lonely. She believes that this feeling of isolation is overwhelming and she needs release from it otherwise she will go mad. She feels that cutting her skin and seeing the blood flow is a kind of ritual she has to undergo to help her cope with all her confusing feelings. She is not sure what these feelings are as she has not explored them in any depth; she feels that she is not able to explain something when she is not sure what it is. She believes that her housemates go to their rooms at night satisfied with the day, and she is left alone to come to terms with the day's events. Usually she feels slighted by others who are too busy or too preoccupied to pay her much attention.

Although she is very good at her studies, she does not believe she will succeed in getting the degree that she feels she deserves. She does not always get very good marks and she worries that her preoccupation with friendships, drinking and going out, cutting and not sleeping very well contribute to her lack of achievement. She is adamant that if she had a partner who was always there for her, then her problems would be over. She concludes that she is very unattractive and dull. She feels that because she is knowledgeable about current affairs and able to quote facts, she is boring and threatening to boys who prefer girls who are fun. She worries that she will disappoint her parents when they realise that their younger daughter to whom they have given a lot is not going to be successful. Although she talks to them about her work difficulties and lack of boyfriends, they are as unable to help her.

A psychodynamic approach to understanding the adolescent's problems
Janice is a young woman who believes that her salvation lies in having someone there for her all the time; she believes that then she will not experience the need to self-harm. This is a narcissistic fantasy, one of fusion with the idealised mother figure who satisfies all the baby's needs. When Janice does not get her wish to have an ever-present protector and provider, she withdraws into herself into a place in her mind of supposed safety and self-sufficiency. But when alone she worries that she has been totally abandoned by everyone, especially this saviour figure, so she experiences isolation, depression and a lack of self-esteem, and the wish to be rescued by this magical figure gets even stronger. She cannot bear the indifference that she feels from her family and friends so she withdraws even more and experiences internal aggressive feelings. These destructive feelings cannot be expressed towards the fantasy mother, who both engulfs the infant and yet is indifferent to it, so the young woman turns her aggression towards herself. She cuts her skin, the container of her body, and in banging her head trying to empty her mind of all thought, she gets some momentary relief from these internal unresolved, irreconcilable psychic conflicts.

Counsellor's assessment
The counsellor listens actively to Janice's presenting problem that she self-harms when she is alone and that she feels rejected, unattractive and depressed.

Janice's self-harming behaviour is assessed for early signs of suicidal risk. Janice is asked how she sees herself in a year's time. The therapist listens to Janice's future plans and is able to assess that Janice has some hope about her future even if it is very vague. If Janice was not able to identify any future plans, then the counsellor would focus on how bleak the young person sees her life, thus eliciting any suicidal plans.

Janice is encouraged to talk of how and when she self-harms. This helps the counsellor to assess the severity of the problem and its frequency; some of the reasons for the self-harming behaviour become evident as she talks of the link between cutting and anger.

Janice is asked to describe how she sees her self-harming behaviour, her feelings of depression, her unattractiveness and aggression.

Janice's history is taken. The history includes early childhood memories and fantasies, parental relationships, sibling rivalries, school experiences, ambitions and her hopes for the future.

A transference comment is made. The counsellor would say something like 'I wonder if between this session and the next you might experience a feeling that I would forget all about you, like you might feel when your mother is preoccupied with your father' or 'I wonder if you experienced the gap between us as me preoccupied with all the other students and I had not thought about you.'

The transference comments are made to elicit whether Janice can work psychodynamically by being able to think symbolically. Can Janice symbolise the therapist as a parent figure? Can she imagine behaving or feeling towards her therapist as she might towards her parents?

The counsellor notes her counter-transference feelings towards Janice. Does she have any feelings of anger or blank spots when with Janice? What does Janice make her feel? Is she accepting of her distress or is she irritated by her need to be loved? These feelings will help the counsellor make meaning of Janice's feelings as they will inform her how Janice is feeling.

A contract is offered to Janice for a period of time and then a review session to elicit the progress of the work.

The ending is talked about in the first session and a link is made between Janice's feelings of rejection by family and friends and the probability that she will feel that her counsellor will also reject her when the contract between them comes to an end.

Counsellor's interventions

Psychodynamic
The aim is to work with the transference and counter-transference to help Janice realise that her self-harming behaviour is linked to unresolved conflicts from her past relationships, especially her parental figures, the internalised punitive father and the internalised ineffective mother. The therapist's interpretations will help Janice become aware that she has a transferential relationship with her. She will eventually recognise that she relates to her therapist in the same way as she related to her care givers during infancy. This understanding will help her recognise that the people in her life do not reject her when they are busy with their own lives; she will perhaps understand that other people, including her parents, do not maliciously cut her out of their lives. This understanding will help her link her self-harming behaviour to her infantile aggressive feelings and in turn help her to modify her behaviour.

Person-centred
The aim of the counsellor is to be empathic, listen actively, show positive regard and be congruent so that Janice can feel her problems are understood. When she feels that her counsellor is there for her, she can begin to reflect on unresolved feelings thus enabling her to make connections between her self-harming behaviour and the way she sees herself.

Cognitive
The aim is to identify and challenge (logically, empirically and pragmatically) Janice's negative cognitive processes, e.g. her belief that everyone is preoccupied with themselves, her feelings of unattractiveness and her feeling that she is boring and uninteresting. It will help her to make a connection between her negative beliefs and her desire to self-harm. If her negative beliefs are successfully challenged, then this will lead to a more positive self-image that in turn should reduce self-harming behaviour.

Counsellor's evaluation

- gradual reduction of self-harming behaviour;
- reduction of distress, anxiety and psychic pain;
- the probability that the depression is reduced;
- loneliness and rejection are no longer linked in Janice's mind;
- improved concentration and better grades in her studies;
- positive self-image and increase in ego strength;
- relationships with family and friends where she can be more communicative;
- an appropriate ending.

Student counselling interview sheets

Name: D.O.B.:

Address:

Tel. No:

Ethnicity: Religion: Gender: F/M

FAMILY BACKGROUND: e.g. type of family, family size, family health, brothers, sisters, etc.

FAMILY RELATIONSHIPS: e.g. relationships with parents/carers, relationships with brothers and sisters, etc.

CHILDHOOD AND SCHOOL HISTORY: e.g. anxieties, fears, depression, bereavement or loss, separation, medical problems, specific learning difficulties, school refusal, truancy, substance abuse, physical, emotional or sexual abuse, referral to external agencies, etc.

COLLEGE HISTORY:

General:

Course(s):

Grades:

Tutor and subject reports:

STUDENT'S SELF-ASSESSMENT: Presenting problems (from student viewpoint): e.g. anxieties, fears, depression, medical problems, substance abuse, physical, emotional or sexual abuse, eating problems, sexual problems, academic under-achievement, absenteeism, personal relationships.

TUTORS', TEACHERS' OR LECTURERS' ASSESSMENT:

COUNSELLOR'S ASSESSMENT, FORMULATION AND RECOMMENDATIONS:

Counsellor's Name: Date:

STUDENT COUNSELLING INTERVIEW SHEET (Parent/Carer)

Parent's/Carer's Name:

Son's/Daughter's Name   D.O.B.:

Address:

Tel. No:

Ethnicity: Religion: Gender: F/M

FAMILY RELATIONSHIPS: e.g. relationships with parents/carers, relationships with brothers and sisters, etc.

CHILDHOOD AND SCHOOL/COLLEGE HISTORY: e.g. son's or daughter's anxieties, grades, fears, depression, bereavement or loss, separation, medical problems, specific learning difficulties, school refusal, truancy, substance abuse, physical, emotional or sexual abuse, referral to external agencies, etc.

PERSONAL RELATIONSHIP: e.g. son's or daughter's ability to make, maintain friendships, appropriateness of friendships, same/opposite sex, isolation, fears/anxieties about friendships.

SON'S/DAUGHTER'S PRESENTATION OF SELF: e.g. dress – appropriateness, make-up, body language.

COUNSELLOR'S COMMENTS AND RECOMMENDATIONS:

Counsellor's Name: Date:

Glossary

This glossary focuses on interventions and intervention-related terms.

Action Plan Order is a court sentence supervised by a Youth Offending Team. The aim is to prevent reoffending. This is to be achieved through reparation, through help with health issues and through encouraging the offender to avoid certain places.

Aggression replacement training is an approach to reduce aggression through training adolescents in pro-social skills. This approach is based on anger control management, self-control techniques and moral training.

Anger management training is an approach aimed at anger control through self-management, and self-instructional and stress-inoculation training.

Anti-social behaviour is defined as behaviour likely to cause harassment, alarm or distress to people who are not living in the same household. Types include graffiti, abusive language, excessive noise, littering, drunkenness and drug dealing.

Anti-Social Behaviour Order (ASBO)/Acceptable Behaviour Contract (ABC) is aimed at stopping anti-social behaviour. An ASBO has legal status whereas an ABC is an informal procedure.

Behaviour support plan is a local education authority (LEA) strategic plan that states how an LEA is going to address the behavioural problems of pupils within its boundaries. The plan aims to improve pupils' life chances by raising achievement, reducing exclusion and raising attendance.

Behavioural approach or behaviour modification is based on the idea that emotional and behavioural problems are mainly the result of maladaptive learning processes, namely classical and operant conditioning. Behavioural interventions are based on classical or operant conditioning and are intended to increase or decrease, modify or extinguish specific, overt and observable behaviours.

Cognitive-behavioural intervention is based on a combination of cognitive and behavioural interventions that focus on changing beliefs, ideas, attitudes, self-efficacy, attributions and expectations that bring about and maintain emotional and behavioural problems. Some examples are cognitive therapy (CT), rational-emotive behaviour therapy (REBT) and problem-solving skills training.

Community Rehabilitation Order is a court order that places an offender under the supervision of a YOT Officer or probation officer. The aim is to stop reoffending through discussing offence, the effects on the offender and others and any other factors such as substance abuse.

Conflict resolution training is designed to train people in negotiation strategies to reduce or eliminate conflicts. The various strategies are distributive, integrative and interactive theories.

Contingency management is a behavioural approach that uses operant techniques to manage the consequences of people's responses in order to change the frequency of those responses.

Counselling is a generic term that encompasses a wide range of counselling approaches including person-centred, behavioural and cognitive behavioural counselling. The counsellor forms a therapeutic alliance with adolescents and, depending on the therapist's particular approach, will help adolescents to reflect upon and change their thoughts, feelings and behaviour.

Detention and Training Order is a court order that aims to stop offending by keeping the offender in a secure environment for half the sentence and the other half under supervision in the community.

Drug therapy is a biologically based approach that regards emotional and behavioural difficulties in part or in full as due to a biochemical dysregulation or dysfunction related to certain neurotransmitters in the brain such as dopamine. A range of drugs exist to treat various disorders. These drugs include antipsychotic (neuroleptic) drugs, anxiolytic drugs and psychostimulants. Some drugs have serious or mild side-effects and some are not prescribed for certain age groups.

Ecological approach regards emotional and behavioural approaches as being the result of reciprocal interactions between people and their social and physical environments and also as a product of their perceptions of those environments. The aim of ecological interventions is to change social and physical environments while at the same time changing perceptions of those environments.

Ecosystemic approach regards emotional and behavioural problems as being the result of negative interactions between people. Ecosytemic interventions are directed at stopping the cycle of negative interactions that serve to maintain emotional and behavioural difficulties by initiating and maintaining a cycle of positive interactions. Negative interactions can occur between teachers and pupils and between parents and adolescents. Specific interventions include reframing, sleuthing, positive connotation of motive and function and symptom prescription.

Education Supervision Order is an order that places a child of school age not being properly educated under the supervision of the LEA.

Family therapy is an approach that regards emotional and behavioural problems as in part or in full the outcome of negative interactions between parents, between parents and children and between siblings. The aim of family therapy is to initiate and encourage positive family interactions that serve to reduce or eliminate emotional and behavioural problems within the family and those that impact on significant others and on institutions external to the family. There are various types of family therapy including strategic family therapy, structural family therapy and Milan family therapy.

Group education plan is an intervention plan that establishes common targets and interventions for pupils in the same group or class.

Group intervention is intervention directed at a group or class and is usually planned where individual intervention is inappropriate, impracticable or uneconomic or where a group or a class as a whole presents problems. Group-directed approaches provide opportunities for sharing problems and experiences and for developing skills and raising self-esteem. There can be a variety of approaches to group work including the behavioural and the cognitive.

Humanistic approach sees emotional and behavioural problems as the result of a negative self-concept and low self-esteem. The aim of a humanistic approach is to help adolescents form positive self-concepts and raise their self-esteem.

Individual education plan (IEP) is a plan drawn up by a school to address a pupil's special educational needs (SEN). It specifies three or four targets and the interventions used to address those needs. The plan also includes success criteria, outcomes and review dates.

Mentoring refers to two approaches to providing advice and support for pupils and students with emotional and behavioural problems. One approach is for school-based learning mentors to work with teachers and pastoral staff in or out of lessons in advising and supporting pupils and students. Another approach is for external mentors who are appropriate role-models to encourage, advise and support pupils and students while at the same time raising their aspirations.

Multi-systemic intervention focuses on systems and their interactions. This approach regards emotional and behavioural problems as not simply a function of the individual alone but also of systemic interactions between individuals, their families and their communities. Interventions are therefore family and community based.

Parent training is an approach based on eliciting the active co-operation of parents in helping to treat their adolescent's emotional and behavioural difficulties. It aims to improve family functioning by equipping parents with coping strategies, particularly those based on behavioural and problem-solving approaches.

Parenting Order is an order offering parents support, guidance and training to help stop their children re-offending and to help them attend school. Parents are required to attend a parenting skills course or a weekly counselling or guidance session.

Pastoral Support Programme (PSP) is a school-based support plan directed at pupils who are at risk of disaffection or exclusion. It is a programme drawn up by the school in collaboration with the pupil, parents/carers, tutors, teachers and external agencies and specifies targets and strategies along with review dates.

Pharmacotherapy is the use of psychoactive drugs for the treatment of disorders such as attention-deficit hyperactivity disorder (ADHD), anxiety, depression and conduct disorders.

Preventive or preventative intervention occurs where interventions are used to prevent emotional and behavioural difficulties from developing in the first place. These include psychoeducation, screening and identification programmes, curricular-based education in schools and colleges using external speakers as well as tutors and teachers, educational visits, advertising campaigns and identification and counselling of adolescents at risk of developing problems.

Problem-solving skills training occurs where adolescents who do not possess adequate problem-solving skills are trained to proceed through structured skills programmes. The aim is to enable adolescents to explore positive and productive alternatives to their current behaviour and to put them into practice.

Psychodynamic approach sees adolescent emotional and behavioural problems as being caused by unconscious conflicts, by unchannelled sexual and aggressive drives and by negative object relations. It also sees emotional maturity as being achieved through the successful transition of developmental stages or phases. In terms of therapy, the concepts of transference and counter-transference are the main therapeutic processes. Transference can be positive or negative and occurs when the adolescent projects feelings, especially the feelings he or she has for parents, onto the therapist. Counter-transference can also be positive and negative and occurs when the therapist projects feelings onto the adolescent. However, where it is not an obstacle to therapy, the therapist can use the counter-transference as a therapeutic tool to increase an understanding of the adolescent's problems. Both forms of transference provide material for the therapist to interpret, and these interpretations help enable the adolescent to gain insight into his or her emotional problems.

Psychoeducation refers to educating people about the nature, content of interventions or strategies, their side-effects and the outcomes of different approaches or therapies used in the treatment of emotional and behavioural problems.

Psychostimulant medication is used in the treatment of ADHD. The main ones are methylphenidate (Ritalin), dexamphetamine (Dexadrine) and pemoline (Cylert).

Psychotherapy refers to the treatment of emotional and behavioural difficulties by psychological methods. To be contrasted with drug therapy where drugs are used to address such difficulties although they can be and are used in combination with psychological approaches.

Rational-emotive therapy focuses on thinking and reasoning and sees emotional and behavioural difficulties as arising from irrational beliefs, interpretations and evaluations of life events. The aim of this approach is to change irrational beliefs through challenging them and then testing them empirically, logically and pragmatically.

Referral Order is a court order that refers an offender to a Youth Offender Panel. The aim of the order is to help stop offending, to help family and friends support the offender and for the offender to hear how the victim feels and ways in which the offender can make reparation. The panel agrees a contract with the offender and the parents.

Relaxation training is a behavioural technique. The aim is to train a person to engage in responses that are incompatible with an undesired response such as anxiety. A person is trained to tense and relax specific groups of muscles.

Reparation Order is a court sentence supervised by the Youth Offending Team. The aim of the order is to prevent further offending and for the offender to understand the effects of the crime on the victim and to make reparation. Elements of reparation include expressing apologies to the victim and carrying out some practical work.

Restorative justice approach is a systematic approach to adolescents and others who have behavioural problems or who commit anti-social and criminal offences. This approach aims to help heal the negative effects of misbehaviour and crime that impact on the offenders themselves, their victims and the community at large. It identifies and takes action to repair the harm done. This may include meeting the victim and discussing the offence, making amends and performing restitution through community service.

School Action is where a class or subject teacher identifies a pupil as having SEN and provides interventions that are additional to or different from those already provided by the school. As part of School Action, an IEP will be drawn up.

School Action Plus is where the class or subject teacher or special educational needs co-ordinator (SENCO) is provided with advice or support from external agencies and specialists so that alternative interventions, additional or different from those already provided by School Action can be implemented.

School-based intervention is a multi-disciplinary and multi-systemic intervention focusing on school systems such as the pastoral system, the referral system, the reward and sanctions system and on classes and groups as well as individuals. Primary prevention focuses on preventing problems emerging in normal populations, e.g. environment change programmes, affective education, and problem-solving skills training. Secondary prevention focuses on identifying early warning signs in order to prevent full-blown problems, e.g. screening and identification programmes and specific types of interventions such as cognitive-behavioural interventions. Tertiary prevention aims to reduce the prevalence of existing problems.

Self-control training See self-management training.

Self-instructional training is a method of developing self-control and involves a gradual change from external to self-control through the internalisation of instructions. It is a staged approach involving modelling the appropriate behaviour, imitation of that behaviour along with self-instruction.

Self-management training focuses on identifying language skills and internal dialogues as a means of exercising self-control. It requires self-recording, self-observation and self-monitoring.

Social learning approach focuses on the influence of inappropriate observational learning and inadequate self-regulation in the formation of emotional and behavioural difficulties. This approach aims to improve self-efficacy and self-regulation through appropriate observational learning and the modelling of appropriate behaviour.

Social skills training aims to address social skills deficits. These deficits are the lack or absence of the necessary skills for interacting appropriately in interpersonal and social situations. Social skills training can include instruction, prompting, shaping, reinforcement, rehearsal, role play, feedback and modelling.

Solution-focused therapy is a form of collaborative brief therapy and concentrates on pursuing the following issues: clarification of the central problem, looking at exceptions to the problem, thinking what the future will be like without the problem and how the skills and resources of adolescents can be used to address their emotional and behavioural problems.

Supervision Order is an order made to help stop offending. The Supervising Officer will give help and advice. The Supervising Officer, with the help of the offender, will work out a supervision plan, the aim being to find out why offending occurs and ways to stop it.

Systemic therapy sees emotional and behavioural difficulties as resulting from interactions between different interconnecting systems such as the individual, the peer group, the family, the school, the neighbourhood and the community. Therefore, any specific therapeutic approach will focus on the formation and maintenance of positive interactions between different systems.

Treatment planning is a treatment plan that includes the following: identifying appropriate interventions for particular emotional and behavioural problems, choosing the most effective setting for those interventions, identifying predisposing, precipitating and perpetuating causes, exploring possibilities for change, considering different viewpoints on the problem, estimating the duration of interventions, establishing success criteria and assessing the level of commitment of those involved.

Whole-School Behaviour Policy (WSBP) is a policy based on the Elton Report that states the principles, methods and procedures involved in managing the behaviour of pupils across the school context. The focus is on classroom management and pastoral and organisational systems and their effects on pupil behaviour. Other policies are connected to or subsumed under WSBPs such as an anti-bullying, anti-racist, anti-sexist policies and SEN policies.

Youth Offending Team (YOT) is a team of youth workers who work with young people in the age group 10 to 17 years who are involved in criminal behaviour. The team might offer the following services: writing pre-sentence reports, parenting order assessments, parenting order supervision, group work, supervision of court orders and young offenders. The team liaise with other agencies such as the police, social services, education, probation, youth services and connections service.

Useful addresses

The following addresses could be used to obtain more information on the issues that might be worrying adolescents, their parents and professionals working with young people. There are a lot more agencies than it is possible to list here. Telephone directories will list self-help groups and agencies in your area. Local libraries might also have lists of useful addresses. Those with Internet access can search for self-help websites; it is important to cross-check the validity of the information and advice offered on such sites.

The aim of the following list is to inform people dealing with adolescent problems that there are agencies that provide advice and support and further treatment where the need arises.

Grateful thanks to Elizabeth Smith and Laura Church for their help in compiling this list.

Helplines

CHILDLINE
Free helpline for children in trouble or danger. 24-hour confidential counselling service.
Childline,
Freepost NATN 1111,
London E1 6BR
0800 1111
www.childline.org.uk

NSPCC
0800 800 500
www.nspcc.org.uk

THE SAMARITANS
This is a 24-hour telephone service for the suicidal, despairing and those passing through personal crisis.

For further information write to Head Office at
The Upper Mill,
Kingston,
Ewell,
Surrey, KT17 2AF
0208 394 8300
Helpline: 0845 790 9090
Befriending by e-mail: jo@samaritans.org
www.samaritans.org.uk

SANELINE
0845 767 8000
www.sane.org.uk

Help with alcohol and smoking

ACTION ON SMOKING AND HEALTH (ASH)
Provides information on smoking and health to the public and health professionals.
0207 739 5902
www.ash.org.uk

AL-ANON
Offers understanding and support for relatives and close friends of problem drinkers.
61 Great Dover Street,
London SE1 4YF
0207 403 0888 (write or phone for your local branch)

ALATEEN
Especially for young people who are affected by an alcoholic relative or close friend.
For details of the nearest group, contact Al-Anon.

ALCOHOLICS ANONYMOUS
A world-wide organisation aiming to help alcoholics to stay sober. No fees; the only requirement is the desire to stop drinking.
For further information:
General Service Office,
PO Box 1,
Stonebow House,
Stonebow,
York YO1 7NJ
General Service Office: 01904 644026
Helpline: 0845 769 7555
London helpline: 0207 833 0022
www.alcoholics anyonymous.org.uk

DRINKLINE
National Alcohol helpline: 0800 776 600
www.wrecked.co.uk

GASP
Provides smoking education resources.
0117 942 5185
gasp@gasp.org.uk
www.gasp.org.uk

SMOKING
Quitline: 0800 02200

TACADE
Produces educational materials for young people on citizenship, alcohol, drugs, smoking and sex education.
0161 836 6850
www.tacade.com

Help with drug problems

FRANK
Organisation that helps young people, their parents and anyone else to know the facts about drugs.
National helpline: 0800 776 600
www.talktofrank.com
There is an e-mail function through the website and if people write Frank will reply.

NARCOTICS ANONYMOUS (NA)
Helpline: 0207 730 0009

NATIONAL DRUGS HELPLINE
0800 776 600

Help with sexual issues

BROOK
Brook 24-hour information line for advice on pregnancy, contraception and abortions: 020 7617 8000
Brook young people's helpline: 0800 018 5023 (Mon–Fri 9 a.m.–5 p.m.)
Brook under-19s sex advice line: 0800 282 930
www.brook.org.uk

THE DRUG RAPE TRUST
01702 317 695
drugrapetrust@hotmail.com

LONDON LESBIAN AND GAY SWITCHBOARD
0207 837 7342

LONDON RAPE CRISIS CENTRE
A telephone service for ALL WOMEN and GIRLS who have been raped, sexually assaulted or abused.
Telephone: Watford: 01923 241 600 or Hounslow: 0208 572 0100

MALE VICTIMS OF SEXUAL ABUSE
Survivors UK
0845 122 1201
www.survivorsuk.co.uk

NATIONAL AIDS HELPLINE
0800 567 123

RAPE AND SEXUAL ABUSE
Rape crisis centre: 0115 900 3560
info@rapecrisis.co.uk
www.rapecrisis.co.uk/support.htm

RAPE CRISES (MALE)
Survivors UK
0207 833 3737

SEXUAL HEALTH HELPLINE
0800 567 123

Help in dealing with anti-social behaviour

BULLYING
Anti-bullying campaign.
0207 378 1446

CRIME VICTIMS
Victim support: 0845 303 0900

CRIMESTOPPERS
0800 555 111
www.crimestoppers.co.uk

GAMCARE
National Association for the Gambling Care
0800 6000 133

KIDSCAPE
Keeping safe, bullying, how to cope.
0207 730 3300
www.kidscape.org.uk

Help with health problems

CHILDREN AND CANCER
0207 696 0900

MENINGITIS RESEARCH FOUNDATION
0808 800 3344

NHS DIRECT
0845 4647

SAD ASSOCIATION
Seasonal Affective Disorder
PO Box 989,
Stenying,
West Sussex BN44 3HG
01903 814 942

Help with emotional problems

CRUSE, BEREAVEMENT CARE
Provides a counselling service, advice and opportunities for social contact. There
are local branches throughout the country.
126 Sheen Road,
Richmond,
Surrey TW9 1UR
0208 940 4818

DEPRESSIVE ALLIANCE
0207 633 0557

EATING DISORDERS ASSOCIATION
103 Prince of Wales Road,
Norwich NR1 1DW
Advice for adults: 0845 634 1414 (Mon–Fri 8.30 a.m.–8.30 p.m.,
Sat 1.30 p.m–4.00 p.m.)
Youth line: 0845 634 7650 (Mon–Fri 4.00 p.m–6.30 p.m.)

EATING DISORDERS ASSOCIATION HELPLINE
01603 621 414
www.edauk.com

MANIC DEPRESSION FELLOWSHIP
0207 793 2600

NATIONAL SELF-HARM NETWORK
0207 916 5472
info@nshn.co.uk
www.nshn.co.uk

OVEREATERS ANONYMOUS
0700 078 4985
www.oagb.org.uk

THE PHOBICS SOCIETY
Helps people who suffer with phobias.
4 Cheltenham Road,
Chorlton-cum-Hardy,
Manchester M21 9QN
0870 7700 456
www.phobics-society.org.uk

Counselling and psychotherapy and psychoanalytic organisations

BRANDON CENTRE
Psychodynamic psychotherapists and clinical psychologists for 12–25-year-olds. Self-referral and referrals from parents, GPs and social services.
26 Prince of Wales Road,
London NW5 3LG
0207 267 4792
e-mail: reception@brandon-centre.org.uk
www.brandon-centre.org.uk

BRENT ADOLESCENT CENTRE
Self-referrals accepted within Brent. Referrals by letter from GP/NHS or other statutory body.
51 Winchester Avenue,
London NW6 7TT
0207 328 0918

BRITISH ASSOCIATION FOR COUNSELLING AND PSYCHOTHERAPY
Can supply information on counselling services nationally and can provide names of individual counsellors and psychotherapist in private practice.
BACP House,
35–37 Albert Street,
Rugby,
Warwickshire CV21 2PJ
01788 550 899

FACES IN FOCUS
Advice and counselling for 13–25-year-olds.
102 Harper Road,
London SE1 6AQ
0207 403 2444

INNER CITY CENTRE
Self-referral for counselling to people over 18.
7 Artillery Lane,
London E1 7PL
0207 247 1589

INSTITUTE OF GROUP ANALYSIS
Self-referral for group, individual, couple and family therapy.
1 Daleham Gardens,
London NW3 5BY
0207 431 4431

LONDON CENTRE FOR PSYCHOTHERAPY
Low-fee scheme psychoanalytic psychotherapy.
32 Leighton Road,
London NW5 2QE
0207 482 2002

THE TAVISTOCK CENTRE
Self-referral or referral by a professional for adolescents with personal problems.
120 Belsize Lane,
London NW3 SBA
0207 435 7111

THE TERRENCE HIGGINS TRUST
To inform, advise and provide help on AIDS and HIV infections; provides welfare, legal and counselling help and support.
Direct helpline for information and support: 0845 1221 200
The sexual health line: 0800 567 123
www.tht.org.uk

WOMEN'S THERAPY CENTRE
Offers psychotherapy, workshops, structured groups to women on issues such as sexual abuse, eating disorders and violent relationships.
10 Manor Gardens,
London N7 6JS
0207 263 6200

WPF COUNSELLING AND PSYCHOTHERAPY
Self-referral or referral from other agencies for adolescents and adults for psychodynamic psychotherapy and counselling.
23 Kensington Square,
London W8 5HN
0207 361 4800

Further referrals

There are many more professional agencies and organisations with qualified staff who work with specific problems that will help relieve the symptoms of the specific problem facing the adolescent.

- In the first instance, a visit to the GP seems the logical step. The GP can refer the adolescent to a specialist clinic or hospital where the adolescent can receive up-to-date treatment.
- Counsellors at schools, colleges and universities can refer an adolescent to an appropriate agency or can give the adolescent information on where to go to find the appropriate help.
- Libraries, Yellow Pages, booklets, leaflets at neighbourhood offices and websites on the Internet have long lists of agencies that support young people. It is important to verify the validity of an agency as well as the information and advice given.

References and further reading

Ashton, R. (2002) *This Is Heroin*, London: Sanctuary Publishing.

Ayers, H., Clarke, D. and Murray, A. (2000) *Perspectives on Behaviour*, 2nd edn, London: David Fulton Publishers.

Ayers, H. and Prytys, C. (2002) *An A to Z Practical Guide to Emotional and Behavioural Difficulties*, London: David Fulton Publishers.

Bandura, A. (1977) *Social Learning Theory*, Englewood Cliffs, NJ: Prentice-Hall.

Bateson, G. (1979) *Mind and Nature: A Necessary Unity*, New York: Dutton.

Beck, A. (1976) *Cognitive Therapy and the Emotional Disorders*, New York: International Universities Press.

Blau, G.M. and Gullotta, T.P. (eds) (1995) *Adolescent Dysfunctional Behaviour*, London: Sage Publications.

Blos, P. (1962) *On Adolescence: A Psychoanalytic Interpretation*, New York: Free Press.

Bowlby, J. (1988) *A Secure Base: Clinical Applications of Attachment Theory*, London: Routledge.

Brandell, J.R. (ed.) (1992) *Counter-Transference in Psychotherapy with Children and Adolescents*, London: Jason Aronson Inc.

British Psychological Society Report (1996) *Attention Deficit Hyperactivity Disorder*, Leicester: The British Psychological Society.

Bronfenbrenner, U. (1979) *The Ecology of Human Development*, Cambridge, MA: Harvard University Press.

Brown, D. and Pedder, J. (1991) *Introduction to Psychotherapy*, 2nd edn, London: Routledge.

Carr, A. (1999) *The Handbook of Child and Adolescent Clinical Psychology*, London: Routledge.

Carr, A. (ed.) (2000) *What Works with Children and Adolescents?* London: Routledge.

Constable, N. (2002) *This Is Cocaine*, London: Sanctuary Publishing.

Cooper, P. and Ideus, K. (1996) *Attention-Deficit/Hyperactivity Disorder*, London: David Fulton Publishers.

Cooper, P., Smith, C.J. and Upton, G. (1994) *Emotional and Behavioural Difficulties*, London: Routledge.

Dallos, R. and Draper, R. (2000) *An Introduction to Family Therapy*, Buckingham: Open University Press.

de Shazer, S. (1985) *Keys to Solution in Brief Therapy*, New York: W.W. Norton.

de Silva, P. and Rachman, S. (1998) *Obsessive-Compulsive Disorder: The Facts*, 2nd edn, Oxford: Oxford University Press.

DfES (2001) *Special Educational Needs Code of Practice*, Annesley: DfES Publications.

Durlak, K. (1995) *School-Based Prevention Programs for Children and Adolescents*, London: Sage Publications.

D'Zurilla, T.J. (1986) *Problem-Solving Therapy*, New York: Springer.

Ellis, A. (1990) *Reason and Emotion in Psychotherapy*, New York: Citadel Press.

Elton Report (1989) London: HMSO.

Emler, N. and Reicher, S. (1995) *Adolescence and Delinquency*, Oxford: Blackwell.

Epanchin, B.C. and Paul, J.L. (eds) (1987) *Emotional Problems of Childhood and Adolescence*, New York: Macmillan.

Erikson, E.H. (1968) *Identity: Youth and Crisis*, New York: Norton.

Feindler, E.L. and Ecton, R.B. (1986) *Adolescent Anger Control*, Oxford: Pergamon.

Findling, R.L., Charles Schulz, S., Kashani, J.H. and Harlan, E. (2001) *Psychotic Disorders in Children and Adolescents*, London: Sage Publications.

Fonagy, P., Target, M., Cottrell, D., Phillips, J. and Kurtz, Z. (2002) *What Works for Whom? A Critical Review of Treatments for Children and Adolescents*, New York: The Guilford Press.

Freud, A. (1958) 'Adolescence', in *The Psychoanalytic Study of the Child*, Vol. 13, New York: International Universities Press.

Frith, C. and Johnstone, E. (2003) *Schizophrenia: A Very Short Introduction*, Oxford: Oxford University Press.

Gilligan, C. (1977) 'In a different voice: women's conceptions of self and morality', *Harvard Educational Review*, 47, 481–517.

Glaser, K. (1981) 'Psychopathological patterns in depressed adolescents', *American Journal of Psychotherapy*, 35, 368–82.

Gordon, R.A. (2000) *Eating Disorders: Anatomy of a Social Epidemic*, 2nd edn, Oxford: Blackwell Publishers.

Harrington, R. (1995) *Depressive Disorder in Childhood and Adolescence*, Chichester: Wiley.

Heaven, P.C.L. (1996) *Adolescent Health*, London: Routledge.

Hill, K. (1995) *The Long Sleep: Young People and Suicide*, London: Virago.

Kalat, J.W. (1998) *Biological Psychology*, 6th edn, Pacific Grove, CA: Brooks Cole Publishing.

Kamphaus, R.W. and Frick, P.J. (1996) *Clinical Assessment of Child and Adolescent Personality and Behaviour*, London: Allyn and Bacon.

Kaplan, H.L. and Sadock, B.J. (1996) *Concise Textbook of Clinical Psychiatry*, 7th edn, London: Williams and Wilkins.

Kassinove, H. (ed.) (1995) *Anger Disorders: Definition, Diagnosis and Treatment*, Washington, DC: Taylor & Francis.

Kegan, R. (1982) *The Evolving Self: Problem and Process in Human Development*, Cambridge, MA: Harvard University Press.

King, N.J., Hamilton, D.L. and Ollendick, T.H. (1994) *Children's Phobias*, Chichester: Wiley.

Kohlberg, L. (1984) *The Psychology of Moral Development*, Vol. 2, San Francisco: Harper & Row.

Kroger, J. (1996) *Identity in Adolescence*, 2nd edn, London: Routledge.

Lemert, E.M. (1972) *Human Deviance, Social Problems and Social Control*, Englewood Cliffs, NJ: Prentice-Hall.

Loevinger, J. (1990) 'Ego development in adolescence', in R.E. Mauss (ed.) *Adolescent Behaviour and Society*, 4th edn, New York: McGraw-Hill.

Luria, A. and Herzog, E. (1985) 'Gender segregation across and within settings', paper presented at the biennial meeting of the Society for Research in Child Development, Toronto.

Marcia, J.E. (1980) 'Identity in adolescence', in J. Adelson (ed.) *Handbook of Adolescent Psychology*, New York: Wiley.

Maslow, A.H. (1954) *Motivation and Personality*, New York: Harper.

Mays, A. (1972) *Juvenile Delinquency, the Family and the Social Group: A Reader*, New York: Longman.

Meichenbaum, D. (1977) *Cognitive-Behavior Modification: An Integrative Approach*, New York: Plenum.

Merton, R.K. (1938) 'Social structure and anomie', *American Sociological Review*, 3, 672–82.

Minuchin, S. (1974) *Families and Family Therapy*, Cambridge, MA: Harvard University Press.

Morgan, C.D. and Murray, H.A. (1935) 'A method for investigating fantasies', *Archives of Neurology and Psychiatry*, 34, 289–306.

Muuss, R.E. (1996) *Theories of* , L

Nicolson, D. and Ayers, selli London: David Fulton Publishers.

O'Connell, B. (1998) *Solution-Focused Therapy*, London: Sage Publications.

Palfai, T. and Jankiewicz, H. (1991) *Drugs and Human Behavior*, Dubuque, IA: Wm. C. Brown.

Pavlov, I.P. (1927) *Conditioned Reflexes*, London: Oxford University Press.

Remschmidt, H. (ed.) (2001) *Psychotherapy with Children and Adolescents*, Cambridge: Cambridge University Press.

Rorschach, H. (1921) *Psychodiagnostics*, Bern: Huber.

Rutter, M. and Giller, H. (1983) *Juvenile Delinquency*, Harmondsworth: Penguin Books.

Rutter, M., Giller, H. and Hagell, A. (1998) *Antisocial Behaviour by Young People*, Cambridge: Cambridge University Press.

Rutter, M., Taylor, E. and Hersov, L. (eds) (1994) *Child and Adolescent Psychiatry: Modern Approaches*, 3rd edn, Oxford: Blackwell Science.

Santrock, J.W. (1996) *Adolescence*, 6th edn, London: Brown and Benchmark.

Schaffer, H.R. (1996) *Social Development*, Oxford: Blackwell.

Selekman, M.D. (1997) *Solution-Focused Therapy with Children*, New York: The Guilford Press.

Sheldon, B. (1995) *Cognitive-Behavioural Therapy*, London: Routledge.

Simos, G. (ed.) (2002) *Cognitive Behaviour Therapy: A Guide for the Practising Clinician*, Hove: Brunner-Routledge.

Spitz, R.A. (1946) *Analytic Depression: Psychoanalytic Study of the Child*, Vol. 2, New York: International Universities Press.

Sutherland, E.H. (1939) *Principles of Criminology*, Philadelphia, PA: Lippincott.

Thomas, G. (2002) *This Is Ecstasy*, London: Sanctuary Publishing.

Thompson, S.B.N. (1993) *Eating Disorders*, London: Chapman and Hall.

Tsuang, M.T. and Faraone, S.V. (1997) *Schizophrenia: The Facts*, 2nd edn, Oxford: Oxford University Press.

Varma, V. (ed.) (1996) *Managing Children with Problems*, London: Cassell Education.

Varma, V. (ed.) (1997) *Violence in Children and Adolescents*, London: Jessica Kingsley Publishers.

von Bertalanffy, L. (1968) *General System Theory*, New York: Brazillier.

Wenar, C. (1994) *Developmental Psychopathology: From Infancy through Adolescence*, 3rd edn, London: McGraw-Hill Inc.

Williamson, D.A. (1990) *Assessment of Eating Disorders*, Oxford: Pergamon Press.

Winkley, L. (1996) *Emotional Problems in Children and Young People*, London: Cassell.

Winnicott, D.W. (1965) *The Maturational Process and the Facilitating Environment*, London: Hogarth Press.